Schools and Community

The Communitarian Agenda in Education

D1322425

James Arthur

with Richard Bailey

London and New York

First published 2000
by Falmer Press
11 New Fetter Lane, London EC4P 4EE

Simultaneously published in the USA and Canada
by Falmer Press
Garland Inc., 19 Union Square West, New York,
NY 10003

Falmer Press is an imprint of the Taylor & Francis Group

© 2000 James Arthur with Richard Bailey

Typeset in Garamond by Taylor & Francis Books Ltd
Printed and bound in Great Britain by Biddles Ltd,
Guildford and King's Lynn

British Library Catal
A catalogue record fo
British Library

Library of Congress Cataloguing in Publication Data
Arthur, James, 1957 –
  Schools and community : the communitarian agenda
  in education / James Arthur with Richard Bailey.
  Includes bibliographical references and index.
  1. Community and school – Great Britain. 2.
  Communitarianism – Great Britain. I. Bailey,
  Richard, 1957– . II. Title.
  LC221.4.G7A78 1999
371.19'0941 – dc21   99 – 39367

ISBN 0–750–70954–5
ISBN 0–750–70955–3 (hbk)

Schools and Community

Contents

Preface

'If the dominant ideology in the 1960s was collectivism, and in the 1980s individualism, the key word as we approach the millennium is *communitarianism*'. So wrote Rabbi Jonathan Sacks in 1997. Certainly the term had gained some political currency in this country with the emergence of New Labour under Tony Blair in the mid-1990s. It was seen at that time as Blair's 'Big Idea' (Phillips 1994). However, in the lead up to the May 1997 General Election, and certainly following New Labour's assumption of power, communitarianism has been hardly audible in the political discourse of the media, the Party and Parliament. That does not necessarily mean of course that communitarian ideas have little or no influence on the policies of a government emphasizing 'modernizing' and 'The Third Way'.

But what exactly is communitarianism? We can get an initial purchase on this somewhat slippery term by considering the familiar triad of individual/community/the state. The community here can be regarded as the multiplicity of formal and informal associations which not only mediate the relationship of the individual to the state but which are also, in a profound sense, *constitutive* of the individual. This notion of the community that includes families, churches, clubs, societies and many other relatively small scale social institutions is not new. It is similar to the 'little platoons' of Edmund Burke.

Our century has been tragically scarred by the excesses of the collectivist politics of Fascism and Communism – both attempts to mould the individual to the dictates of the State. More recently, political ideologies based on liberal or libertarian individualism are increasingly seen as inimical to the well-being of society. It is hardly surprising then, at the present *fin de siècle*, that an emphasis on community should re-emerge as a possible route to secular salvation.

It would be quite wrong to suppose that communitarianism is a monolithic political concept. The term, as this book so clearly shows, has a variety of nuances. Communitarians can and do occupy different positions on the liberal–conservative continuum. There are nevertheless sufficient 'family resemblances' between the different stances for one to talk intelligibly and usefully about communitarianism.

Communitarianism has a special significance for schools and those who work in them. A school is necessarily a community – a community of pupils, teachers, parents. It is also, particularly through its parents, linked to the local community beyond its walls. A key function of schools is to help prepare pupils to become full participants in their community and eventually in society at large. In that way schools are inevitably committed to the 'common good' – a notion that has perhaps become somewhat occluded in an age of rampant individualism.

The way in which we currently seek to understand, justify and improve schools is heavily dominated by the language of markets and managerialism, which many consider increasingly sterile and dehumanizing. Ideas of communitarianism tapping, as they do, other ethical discourses and traditions may provide a salutary corrective and even reinvigorate the nature of educational debate.

James Arthur's book is to be commended for two very important reasons. First, it provides the general reader with a very accessible introduction to communitarianism and its significance for social policy. It is based on a very thorough reading of the existing literature and its excellent bibliography will be invaluable to those knowing something already of the topic and who wish to know more.

Second, the book is surely amongst the first to offer a sustained analysis of a possible 'communitarian agenda in education'. For me, two things of particular significance emerge from this agenda. The first is a recognition of the very distinctive contribution that can be made by religiously affiliated schools. Such schools often seem to add something over and above that found in other schools. This may be the consequence of their having an extended community of pupils, parents and church broadly united by a set of common beliefs. In effect these schools embody a religious communitarian ethos that provides a powerful coherence to their educational mission.

The majority of schools, however, do not have a religious affiliation and must find their justification and coherence through a more secular rationale. This leads me to my second agenda point which is that 'education for citizenship' is a main contender for such a rationale. Certainly the government's intention is that a place will be found for citizenship education in the curriculum of all pupils. The book provides a very timely examination of this still relatively unfamiliar curricular component and its relationship to communitarian notions such as the common good.

The communitarian agenda is no universal panacea for all the problems of schools and the book, although sympathetic to the agenda, wisely eschews a doctrinaire position for or against. James Arthur is rather its 'critical friend'. What he has done is to bring an important but multi-faceted concept to our attention and, in doing so, has enriched contemporary educational debate. And the book will undoubtedly provoke debate. The final sentence of the book is as good a starting off point as any for such a debate:

> The problem with the communitarian agenda for education is that it promises more than exclusive State institutional schooling can possibly deliver.

Brian Wilcox
Honorary Professorial Fellow
Department of Educational Studies
University of Sheffield

Introduction

It is typical of our time that the more doubtful we are about philosophy, the more certain we are about the value of education. That is to say, the more doubtful we are about whether we have any truth, the more certain we are (apparently) that we can teach it to children.

(G. K. Chesterton, *Illustrated London News* 12 January 1907)

This book does not align itself with any specific communitarian movement or agenda, principally because of the great diversity of beliefs and policy positions adopted by those who describe themselves as communitarians. This diversity of policy positions was well illustrated when Dr Richard Bailey and I were invited in 1998 by Professor Amitai Etzioni to speak at the fifth annual Communitarian Network Conference on Character Building in Washington DC. The conference dramatically demonstrated the great diversity of positions adopted by communitarians and those who are closely allied with or sympathetic to communitarian modes of thinking. It appeared that the rhetorical power of communitarian speakers at the conference exceeded their ability to expound their public policy arguments and theses clearly. There seemed to be as many communitarian positions as communitarian speakers. It felt very much as if the communitarian movement was in its early stages of development and that there were no blueprints, only items on the agenda for discussion.

There are really only versions of communitarianism and so it would be illogical to speak of '*the* communitarian view': rather 'the communitarian perspective' or 'communitarianisms' are more appropriate for the discussion in this book. Etzioni (1993:254) says: 'a communitarian perspective does not dictate particular policies'. This may well be the case because, while New Labour appear to reflect a communitarian perspective, it is often difficult to identify the specific policy proposals

1

that emerge as distinctly communitarian. There is also a real difficulty in trying to categorize communitarianism on the contemporary political spectrum, which is probably why it often enjoys bipartisan political appeal and attracts a range of commitments.

Nevertheless, these diverse communitarian ideas can offer an important and even vigorous challenge to contemporary views of education, and there exists a body of core principles within communitarian thinking that can make a positive contribution to the debate about national education policy. This book is therefore sympathetic to, but not uncritical of communitarian thinking on education. It does not accept the more radical communitarian views that reject individual civil and political rights and seek to replace these with teleological talk about the good of communities or with vague talk about group rights. The discussion within the book is more comfortable with the moderate communitarian positions which assert that political and civil rights are important and must form the basic framework within a democratic society, but that they do not have the priority that modern society often gives them. In other words, there are cases in which particular individual rights may be restricted in scope for the sake of the 'common good' of a community. Recent communitarian thinking can certainly be provocative and exciting, but it is recognized that there are serious ambiguities as to the nature and import of communitarian arguments within a pluralist society. The attempt in this book is to articulate and describe some basic communitarian positions and to demonstrate that they have an important contribution to make in the debate on education. The subject matter of this text is limited and does not cover the entire range of philosophical and political points that are emerging from the communitarian literature. Consequently, 'liberalism' is generally used in the text to highlight communitarian perspectives, and in the process some liberal ideas may appear to have been caricatured as a contrasting position. Essentially, liberalism is defined in this text as the dominant ideology in Britain which is distinguished by the huge importance it attaches to the civil and political rights of individuals. The dominant and popular language of liberalism remains concerned with individual rights, freedom and equality of opportunity.

It should also be clearly emphasized that the material in this book does not presume to talk about 'the communitarian position' far less provide the reader with a definitive communitarian approach to education. I do not accept that you can talk about 'communitarian democracy', 'communitarian citizens', 'communitarian politics', 'communitarian values', 'communitarian governance', and even 'communitarian faith' to name but a few of the many curious 'positions' adopted by writers on communitarianism. Communitarianism has not developed in a unitary enough fashion to warrant the use of these terms without very serious qualification. Many writers on the subject work at a rhetorical level and their 'communitarianisms' have a high level of use, but a low level of meaning. A more cautious approach is adopted here in view of the complexity and problematic nature of communitarianism itself.

In spite of the lack of clarity of some of their arguments, communitarian thinkers can provide some useful insights about the possibility of an alternative vision of education and schooling to those views that are dominant in contemporary education practice in England and Wales. Communitarians have made a strong case for taking the value of community seriously and consequently they have recognized the limitations of the value placed on autonomy in our education system. One of the reasons why communitarian ideas have attracted people from all sides of the political spectrum is because of their explicit appeal to community. The modest attempt in this short volume is to articulate some of the central themes in communitarian thought in regard to education, and it is offered as an introduction to teachers and those concerned with the education system. Readers will not find in this text any definite advocacy of one position. The following chapters will provide a sketch of the debates and connections between communitarianism and education and will attempt to outline what the communitarian agenda might be for schools.

Chapter One considers the meaning of communitarianism with a particular focus on unpacking the communitarian concepts of the community. The chapter identifies some of the key themes in the liberal-communitarian debate. Chapter Two, written by Richard Bailey and me, explores the changing face of family life and structure in England and Wales and discusses what communitarian policies on the moral education of children within families might look like. Chapter Three looks at communitarian views of education in schools, examining the themes of character/values education and community service within the school curriculum. Chapter Four continues the examination of the school curriculum from the perspective of citizenship education and the common good, and the school is located as a civic institution. Chapter Five considers how various communitarian writers understand the role and position of religiously affiliated schools in modern society. In Chapter Six, Richard Bailey gives consideration to a number of case studies of schools that illustrate some of the practices of a community-based education and give some insight into what communitarian approaches to education might look like. The conclusion summarizes the central agenda items for education of both the communitarian movement and various communitarian thinkers.

I would like to thank Professor Brian Wilcox, Jon Davison, Professor Carl Parsons, Hugh Walters, Simon Hughes and John Moss for reading and commenting on early drafts of this manuscript. In addition, thanks to the staff and community of the three schools visited by Dr Richard Bailey to interview staff and collect information for Chapter Six.

James Arthur
Canterbury
February 1999

1 Communitarianism

For many the instant connotation of community is a local residential community, that is, a small and bounded territory. This can be reduced in size to a district, an electoral ward, a neighbourhood or a street. It can be expanded to a village, town or city, a county, a region, a nation, a continent, a world. This spatial conception of community is of self-evident significance, but it far from exhausts the conception of community. It ignores the small communities which we most value – family, kinship networks, friendship groups. We are also members of institutional communities – classes, year groups, houses, teams, and so on in schools ... For many people institutional forms such as churches, clubs, parties are expressions in community of their religious, leisure and political interests. Any adequate conception of the community must include all of these, and more, if it is to be the foundation of a compulsory curriculum. Three things are at once apparent: we all belong to multiple communities; our community membership often changes; the communities of which we are members may be in conflict with one another.

(David Hargreaves 1982:135)

As has been said in the Introduction, there are almost as many communitarianisms as communitarians. It is possible to identify socialist, conservative and liberal communitarians within the United Kingdom alone. Essentially, however, it may be helpful to view the movement as divided into two main streams. One would be seen (and see itself) as a corrective to, and development of classical Anglo-Saxon liberalism, extending and deepening its social context. The other stream would be in different ways more hostile, drawing on Catholic or socialist elements for a more fundamental critique of individualism. The position is not as clear cut as this, with many thinkers drawing on elements from both streams. This rather amorphous state of development in communitarian thinking makes it an interesting and useful object of study since at the moment it is capable of development into several different broad conclusions about the nature of society and its members, and how the two should relate to each other.

Communitarianism is a philosophical stance originating from academia and developed from a critique of certain elements of liberal individualism by such people as Michael Sandel, Alasdair MacIntyre, Charles Taylor, Michael Walzer and John Gray. Communitarianism is therefore a rather loose grouping which holds that the community, rather than the individual or State, should be at the centre of our analysis and our value system. The term has not yet been systematized in political philosophy, but has been popularized by Amitai Etzioni whose particular version of communitarianism has had a considerable influence on both the Democrats in the USA and the New Labour Party in Britain. For a number of years, Tony Blair has raised the concepts of community, responsibility and duty, all central to communitarian thinking, to pivotal positions in the Labour Party manifesto. In America there has been some popular appropriation of the term communitarianism by what amounts to a political movement. This communitarian movement is led by Etzioni himself, the media-styled 'prophet of communitarianism'. Since the 1970s general theories of communitarianism have begun to challenge existing political theories. Indeed, the central contemporary debate in political philosophy has been that between liberalism and the communitarians (Miller 1990, Carey 1992, Daleney 1994). As a consequence, definitions and understandings of communitarianism have generally arisen out of this communitarian/liberal debate. Within this debate Patrick Neal and David Paris (1990) observe that: 'The competing positions are often difficult to characterise (or, sometimes, even to distinguish) and it is often unclear what would be the theoretical and or practical significance of affirming one position over the other'.

At one level, there appear to be two distinct groups that are normally referred to as communitarians. The first group, who will be labelled 'communitarian theorists', engage in debate with liberalism but do not generally advocate specific public policy statements. The second group, the 'public philosophy communitarians', are similarly critical of liberalism and other dominant political stances, and seek a communitarian perspective on legal, social and educational public policies. While there is a general connection between these two groups, there are also important differences and so it is worthwhile to distinguish between them. This chapter is concerned with both groups in an attempt to understand how they define communitarianism, and goes on to consider recent work by political theorists like John Gray, who have begun to bridge the gap between academic debate and practice. It concludes with the application of the language and approaches of communitarianism by the New Labour of Tony Blair and his colleagues.

Community: Understanding Communitarianism

'Community' is the key concept in any understanding of communitarianism. Communitarians generally make several claims about the nature of persons and human identity not least that persons are embedded in communities. They claim that the self is constituted to some extent through a community that provides shared values, interests or practices. A person's individual values are formed in the social context of these communities and often pursued through communal attachments (Wil Kymlicka 1993). Communitarians emphasize the embedded status of the person and almost all communitarians are, therefore, united around a conception of human beings as 'integrally related to the communities of culture and language that they create, maintain and sustain' (Stephen Mulhall and Adam Swift 1996:162). The separate individual does not make up the basic moral unit of society in this scheme of things, but rather is attached to other individuals in community on whom he or she is somewhat dependent. The appeal of communitarianism is obvious since there is a growing perception that there has been an erosion of communal life in contemporary society, and that this is associated in some way with a decline in standards of behaviour and relationships and increasing crime and social exclusion (the literature on this matter is huge; see, for example, Anthony Giddens 1998, Bright 1997, Wilson 1993). However, we need to look at what the communitarians mean by community since what has been said already could have been said from the perspective of contemporary liberalism.

Daniel Bell (1993:93ff) helps develop an understanding of the implications of the communitarian concept of community. He agrees that deeply felt attachments to a number of communities help constitute a person's identity. This allows that person to experience life as bound up with the good of these communities. These *constitutive communities* define the sense of who we are and provide the largely unconscious background to our being in the world of thinking, acting and deciding. Daniel Bell argues that we cannot easily shed what we are since we are principally connected with these constitutive features of

7

our identity in a way that often resists articulation. To reject them can lead to a potential crisis of identity or a form of disorientation. Bell suggests that it is possible to answer the question of what these constitutive communities are by asking a very simple question: 'Who are you?' (Bell 1993:97). The answer might involve such elements as family name, nationality, language, culture and religion – all of which relate to the community in which people grow. It is important to say that Bell does not have in mind a monolithic society where everyone has the same commitments and simply conforms, but he does claim that there is no such thing as the 'unencumbered self'. In other words, no individual can find an identity apart from others. This line of thought about the centrality of the community obviously places limits on individual freedom and autonomy through emphasis on our attachments to the community. This is the understanding of community, perhaps best popularized as 'it takes a village to raise a child', which has caused a number of liberals to reformulate some of their ideas on education.

One of the basic premises of recent communitarian thinking is that modern Western society has lost a sense of social solidarity. It lacks the communal dimensions that might unite people around a conception of what is good or worthwhile to pursue in life. Therefore, communitarians argue that there should be an attempt to forge a new equilibrium between rights and responsibilities. Libertarian individualism, they claim, has been destructive of the community as a result of a shift too far in the direction of individual rights and away from duty and responsibility to the people with whom we live. The philosophy teaches that both State solutions and the market are inadequate if they stand alone, since their value lies solely in the contributions they can make to the quality of life. John Gray, who was at one time associated with the free market economics and policies of the Thatcher years, has more recently conceded that the spread of the market system ought to be limited where it is likely to conflict with existing 'local' traditions or be harmful to the development of community and social inclusion and as he concludes (1993:63): 'the market is made for humans, not humans for the market'. Communitarian perspectives are bound up with the concepts of fraternity, solidarity, civic pride, social obligation and tradition, and are seen as corrective of the recent 'cult of the individual'.

Etzioni (1995a:260), borrowing terms and ideas from Catholic social teaching, i.e. 'common good', 'solidarity' 'subsidiarity', (Anthony Giddens 1998:112), describes his communitarian approach to responsibility as a principle of subsidiarity in which the primary responsibility belongs to the individual nearest the problem. If a solution cannot be found, then the responsibility moves to the family. If there is still no solution, then the community, then, and only then, when no solution is possible at all, should the State be involved. In other words, there needs to be a renewed emphasis on an ethical base for political action that encourages the intermediate institutions that stand between the individual and the State: family, schools, trade unions, religious groups, the neighbourhood and voluntary organizations. It is not surprising then that communitarians have consistently accused liberalism of resting on an overly individualistic conception of the person, a conception that does not sufficiently take account of the importance of community for personal identity and moral thinking. While communitarians claim that we can critically examine our attachments to communities, they uphold the view that some attachments are so fundamental to our identity we cannot set them aside without harmful costs to ourselves and the community.

The Communitarian Theorists

In the 1970s liberal political thought flourished and four books in particular advanced the liberal cause: John Rawls' *A Theory of Justice* (1972), Ronald Dworkin's *Taking Rights Seriously* (1978a), Robert Nozick's *Anarchy, State and Utopia* (1977) and Bernard Crick's *In Defence of Politics* (1962). These texts have largely defined the agenda for the debate between liberalism and communitarianism (Wallach 1987). These books placed an emphasis on individual liberty, on rights and on distributive justice which caused some commentators to refer to them as 'rights theorists'. For these liberal authors society should provide a framework for its members to choose their own values and ends. The function of the State is simply to promote the capacity of each and every individual to decide for him or herself what is good or worthwhile. Society does not choose in advance what the common good would be, since society is not intended to have a vision of the good. The State should, therefore, not reward or penalize particular conceptions of the good life held by its members. The State simply provides a neutral framework within which potentially conflicting conceptions of the good can be pursued. This is the liberalism of much of our contemporary society – we live it.

Rawls, in particular, attempted to establish a philosophical method that would help us adjudicate moral and political conflict in our democratic methods so that we can preserve individual rights. This is the liberal thesis of the primacy of the right over the good. In other words, the pursuit of the good by individuals has only to be constrained by the impartial principles of justice that everyone finds reasonable. The response of the communitarian theorists has been to argue that Rawls and other liberal thinkers have constructed a liberal theory that is too abstract and individualistic, ignoring the moral and social nature of human beings. Two major attacks are made against these liberals by communitarian theorists that are summarized by Avineri and De-Shelit (1992:2) in the following way: first, that the premises of individualism, such as the rational being who chooses freely, are wrong or false and that the only way to refer to individuals is in their social context; second, that the premises of individualism give rise to morally unsatisfactory consequences. Communitarians make it clear that our attachment to communities is not voluntary, that social attachments are not normally chosen ones (for example, family, nationality, etc.), and that our upbringing and the values we adopt and live by are often acquired involuntarily rather than being a matter of rational choice by the individual.

For Michael Sandel (1994), liberalism, insofar as it is individualistic, is the politics of rights, while communitarianism is the politics of the common good. Sandel explains the liberal position in the following way:

> the right is prior to the good, and in two senses: the priority of the right means, first, that individual rights cannot be sacrificed for the sake of the general good (in this it opposes utilitarianism), and, second, that the principles of justice that specify these rights cannot be premised on any particular vision of the good life (in this it opposes teleological conceptions in general).

He rejects the liberal view of man as a free and rational being in favour of the Hegelian conception of man being historically conditioned. For him there is no such thing as an unencumbered self since the self is always constituted through community. Sandel (1994:16) claims that we should give up the politics of rights in favour of a politics of the common good. The danger that liberals see in this line of argument is that it may assume common interests within communities when none exist. It may, as a result of such an assumption, marginalize dissent within a democratic society in favour of an ideal of the 'common good'; a common good, which in all probability, may favour the values and interests of the most articulate and powerful groups in society. Amy Guttman (1987:121), for example, has said that 'the good society of the old critics was one of collective property ownership and equal political power; the good society of the new critics is one of settled traditions and established identities'. Likewise, Derek Phillips (1993:173) warns of the dangers involved in inflexible and backward-looking community-based politics, listing racism, sexism, exclusion and forced emigration and exile as methods that have been adopted by communities in the past to establish themselves.

Some communitarian theorists use historical theses of idyllic communities in past periods to support their moral and political theories. David Popenoe (1994:27) is most explicit in terms of policy implications. He calls for a return to 'Natural Communities' which are small, village-like groups protected, to some extent, from intrusion by outsiders. According to this overtly anachronistic vision, mobility of residents would be reduced, diversity would be resisted and strict moral standards would be enforced, all in the name of social stability and community. Derek Phillips' research, however, has seriously undermined the strength of these claims by offering a wealth of evidence that traditional communities, including the exemplars of Classical Athens, the Middle Ages and America at the time of the Founding Fathers, which have been very popular among communitarian writers, rarely manifest standards of justice, equality and liberty that would be acceptable in modern society.

Mary Ann Glendon (1991) has challenged the rights-based thinking of liberals and has detailed the limits of its resulting 'legalism' in her book *Rights Talk*, calling for a moratorium on the manufacturing of new rights. She believes that the liberal position on human rights has shifted from: 'I can do what I want as long as I do not hurt others', to 'I can do what I want because I have a right to do so'. She thus rejects Ronald Dworkin's (1978a) absolute emphasis on the priority of rights, and in particular his statement that: 'if someone has a right to do something, then it is wrong for the government to deny it to him even though it would be in the general interest to do so' (ibid.:269). There is an increasing tendency to define the relation of self to others and to society as a whole in terms of rights and to judge whether one has been treated properly or whether one has had one's rights fairly defended. This unbalanced emphasis upon rights, she believes, militates against the common good of any society, because it ignores the social costs of decisions made by individuals.

Even more critical has been the work of Alasdair MacIntyre (1981,

1987) who believes that liberalism rests on a series of mistaken ethical views about human nature and that it understates the role of tradition and community in the development of individuality and moral authority. For MacIntyre, individuals understand their lives by looking at their actions within their own story, a 'narrative'. But this narrative converges with those of other people, who come to be part of one's own narrative. Thus an understanding of oneself can be attained only in the context of the community that sets up the form and shape as well as the circumstances and the background of these narratives. Our identities are constructed by the stories we tell ourselves and our virtues and values are prescribed by the very nature of the specific social practices in which they function. MacIntyre does not think that the State can have any conception of the good; he follows the Aristotelian line that justice is rooted in a community whose bond is a shared understanding both of the good for man and the good of that community. He rejects the liberal view of the individual and his rights as paramount above society. In the context of liberalism we have, according to MacIntyre, no rational principles for ranking, synthesizing and choosing goods that means that moral judgement is reduced to expressions of personal approval or disapproval. Both Sandel and MacIntyre provide a theoretical basis for understanding a communitarian concept of the community. For these theorists, the elements that make up a community are shared history, shared practice, shared meanings, shared discourse, a common tradition and common ideas about life together.

Another contribution to the debate was *Habits of the Heart* (1985), in which Robert Bellah and his colleagues attempt to challenge conceptions of community. Drawing heavily upon the framework provided by MacIntyre's *After Virtue*, these writers are convinced that individuals have become increasingly detached from their social and cultural contexts, and they seek to reverse this trend through the renewal of community. *Habits of the Heart* provides a definition of community that includes both a territorial and relational dimension: territorial in the sense that a community is located within a specific geographical area, and relational in the sense that community exists when there is a quality to the relationships and associations among people. Bellah and his colleagues place great emphasis on the relational aspects of community and also emphasized the interdependence of these relationships. Such a community would have a community of memory and tell its story or narrative of common values which are deeply rooted in the history of the community. Members of the community would involve themselves in shared practices and manifest loyalty and obligations that keep the community alive. There would be a sense of solidarity with everyone else in the community and a relationship of reciprocity. Phillips (1993:14) draws his definition of community from this dimension of the communitarian position: 'A community is a group of people who live in a common territory, have a common history and shared values, participate together in various activities, and have a high degree of solidarity'.

In reading the literature on the liberal/communitarian debate, it is the case that liberals and communitarians sometimes recommend very similar policies. Since there can be so much in common between both positions the question arises as to whether or not it is possible to equate them? While Guttman criticizes MacIntyre and Sandel, she sees communitarianism as supplementing liberal values, not supplanting them. It is merely a help for liberalism to discover a politics that combines community with a commitment to liberal values (Guttman 1987:133). After all, no comprehensive political philosophy can seriously ignore the social aspects of everyday life, and this must be the case for liberalism, despite its emphasis upon the individual. On the other hand, others have stressed that communitarian ideas can address certain fundamental errors within traditional liberalism. As Moody says:

> The communitarian complaint is not that people as conceived of by liberalism will not co-operate or act for the common good, but rather that they do so for the wrong reasons, simply from self interest or as a matter of obligation. But communitarianism sees public life as a constitutive feature of human identity, and thus a necessary part of a good life and valuable for its own sake, not simply as an instrument for purely private ends.
>
> (quoted in Daleney 1994:97)

This is why a number of liberals, such as John Gray, have conceded points to communitarian theorists by revising or explaining some of their positions (compare, for example, Gray's views in 'The Undoing of Conservatism' – included as Chapter 7 in Gray 1995b – with his open adoption of communitarianism in *After Social Democracy*, Gray 1996). The basic criticism of liberalism is that it places the individual in a sovereign position with no substantive human good that transcends his or her choices, against which the communitarian theorists turn to concepts of community, the common good and virtue. Interestingly, few of the communitarian theorists say much about practical communitarian politics. This may be because they disagree with the political conclusions drawn by some in the communitarian movement. Alternatively, it may simply be that these writers refuse to place the political realm at the centre of their vision or task, since they are more concerned to criticize the various forms of liberal political philosophy.

The Public Philosophy Communitarians

A new dimension to the communitarian debate emerged in 1990 as a result of a meeting of fifteen social philosophers, ethicists, and social scientists at which they discussed the establishment of a group to explore a number of social matters affecting society. This group included Amitai Etzioni who in January 1991 launched, as editor, a communitarian journal entitled *The Responsive Community: Rights and Responsibilities*. The group did not wish to describe itself either as liberal or conservative since it believed these terms were increasingly outdated. By November, the group had issued a communitarian platform in the form of a 14-page document summarizing their approach and listing their basic objectives (Etzioni 1995a, 1997). The statement was supported by a large number of influential individuals, representing both academic institutions and voluntary organisations, and included the statement:

> Neither human existence nor individual liberty can be sustained for long outside the interdependent and over-lapping communities to which we all belong. Nor can any community long survive unless its members dedicate some of their attention, energy, and resources to shared projects. The exclusive pursuit of private interest erodes the network of social environments on which we all depend, and is destructive to our shared experiment in democratic self-government. For these reasons, we hold that the right of individuals cannot long be preserved without a communitarian perspective. A communitarian perspective recognises both individual human dignity and the social dimension of human existence.

Community was clearly to be the central concept in their new movement, supported by traditional conceptions of the family, values and education. These communitarians, led by Etzioni, returned to the classical sociology represented by Emile Durkheim (1858–1917). It was an attempt to spread the message from academia to influence American public opinion by turning theoretical communitarianism into a public philosophy.

More recently, Britain has witnessed the emergence of its own communitarian movement, although it is clearly still in its infancy. Its first Position Paper seems to suggest that its stance and rationale are generally similar to that of Etzioni's group. In order to combat a perceived moral and social decline, they argue, it is necessary to build 'democratic communities'. Such communities are characterized by an open and rational exchange of ideas necessary to address the urgent problems facing society, a shared sense of responsibility for the well-being of others, all guided by an awareness of the importance of cooperative action in the sustenance of the common good (Henry Tam 1998:3–4). Compared to theorists like MacIntyre and Sandel, the public philosophy communitarians have greatly expanded the policy implications dimension. The communitarian theorists challenge the individualistic liberal opposition to the common good, while this new movement has expanded this notion by adding questions about the balance between responsibility on an individual and social level and promoting the idea of pluralism bounded by a core of shared values. Etzioni (1997:9) places his position against the background of a traditional political division: 'Between individuals, who champion autonomy, and social conservatives, who champion social order, lies communitarianism, which characterises a good society as one that achieves balance between social order and autonomy'. This seems to be an attempt to shore up values, institutions and responsibilities and communities without being overly conservative or dogmatic. Another way of looking at it would be to suggest that communitarianism is really only a very 'compromised' third way.

Etzioni's particular version of communitarianism is essentially a political movement – with him firmly established as the party leader – seeking to affect public opinion and policy. His communitarian movement claims to be non-partisan, but it is intimately connected with American politics. However, it is difficult to see what Etzioni has actually added to communitarian theory. His ideas about the restoration of community are beset with conceptual obfuscation and his writing on communitarianism is characterized by strongly ideological tendencies. His writings tend to view community as an uncontestable good, but, of course, this is not the case. Communities in general, and particularly some of the 'Natural Communities' that have been advocated, have a real potential to exclude and discriminate. It is not therefore surprising that he has many critics within academia (cf. Demain and Entwhistle

1998) and that few intellectual communitarian theorists overtly support Etzioni's movement. Nonetheless, a number of influential thinkers and writers have felt sufficient sympathy with the general communitarian perspective to contribute to the journal, *The Responsive Community*, including the likes of John Gray, William Damon, William Sandel, Ann Glendon, and Daniel Bell as well as those less associated with the position, such as Ralf Dahrendorf, Carl Sagan and Daniel Goleman.

MacIntyre is viewed with respect, but viewed nevertheless as a social conservative by Etzioni. In order to distinguish his movement clearly from claims that he is a liberal in conservative clothes, Etzioni has modified the name of his movement – 'responsive communitarians'. Etzioni has made it clear that his communitarianism is responsive to all members of a community and that it definitely is not the same as being majoritarian. In a sense, Etzioni has presented communitarianism as an ally of liberalism against State coercion. Values are central to this public philosophy communitarianism and there is much talk of the restoration of the community being their core mission (Etzioni 1995a:12). In his most recent book *The New Golden Rule* (1997), Etzioni elaborates his thoughts by asking two basic questions: How should a communitarian society operate in practice? What values are necessary to achieve stronger community ties? Etzioni offers a secularized version of the well-known biblical adage 'do unto others as you would have them do unto you'; it becomes 'respect and uphold society's moral order as you would have society respect and uphold your autonomy to live a full life'. In other words, the individual should empathize with someone affected by his or her actions. The focus is still on the imbalance between individual rights and social responsibility, but in addition Etzioni believes that *order* and *autonomy* in some sort of balance create good communities. However, he advocates very basic kinds of virtues (*virtues* and *values* are often used by Etzioni to mean the same thing) on the general understanding that members of a community act in a way that is considered right, even if that means giving up something which is considered to be desirable. Consequently, excessive liberty presents a threat to society, due to its omission of duty. Core values are essential to this model, and it is not surprising that many public philosophy communitarians place enormous importance upon schools, not least for the valuable role they can play in transmitting core values to the next generation. For Etzioni, this function is their most important mission.

Communitarian Liberalism

The communitarians have received a mixed reception among academics and policy-makers. Many have acclaimed their emphasis upon the community, with the range of understandings that word brings. There does seem to be a general acceptance that it is important and worthy to live our lives with a thought and feeling for the well-being of others, and many writers have called for a corrective to the excessive individualism of recent years. However, many of the practical policy implications suggested by the public philosophy communitarians seem to be resting upon unsteady foundations. The call for 'Natural Communities' is a case in point. There may well be an intuitive appeal to the idea of the serenity and order of a bygone age in which people grew, lived and died within a community characterized by reciprocity and stability. Perhaps it does not matter very much that such communities seem not to have existed, at least in the idyllic form portrayed by communitarians (as Phillips 1993 appears to show). Jean-Jacques Rousseau might have argued that the issue is rather unimportant, since it is the *concept* of these communities that is most important. In other words, stories of traditional communities can be viewed as thought-experiments, in which the elements of society that lead to cooperation, order and stability are writ large, and contrasted with the changes that lead to selfishness, disorder and anarchy.

The above only stands serious inspection if it is acknowledged that it is an idea that challenges current assumptions. In order for any social policy to deserve consideration, let alone implementation, it must satisfy some standards of practicality. While it is perfectly reasonable to be concerned with the effects of an excessive individualism and anti-social behaviour, we cannot model our policy upon forms of community life that do not exist for the great majority of people today. A weakness identified by critics of liberalism, as well as a large number of liberals themselves, is that liberalism ignores the community dimension to politics at its peril. Indeed, Richard Dworkin (1978b:260), one of the more forceful defenders of the rights-based approach to political philosophy, has acknowledged the need for liberalism to come to terms with the individual's culture and influences, as without it a liberal theory of education, to use the case at hand, becomes impossible:

> It is very important for liberals to develop a theory that would make a distinction here between enriching the choice available to people and enforcing a choice upon people. The crucial idea, it

seems to me, is the idea of imagination. It does seem to me that liberalism is rather weak at this point and needs a theory of education and a theory of culture-support that it does not have. That, I think, is part of the answer to the question: 'What must political theory do?'

A number of liberal writers such as John Gray, Joseph Raz and Isaiah Berlin have recognized the omission of community from liberal theory, and have gone some way to offer a form of communitarian liberalism that maintains the place of autonomy and individual decision-making so fundamental to the Western way of life and conception of well-being, while placing these aspects within the context of community. That Gray, in particular, has come to advocate a communitarian position is interesting, as in his earlier writing he was one of the most articulate defenders of the free market and classical liberalism, and in recent years has moved to become one of Tony Blair's centre-left 'gurus' (cf. David Willetts 1996). Robert Nash (1997:57) calls these communitarians 'civic-liberal communitarians' because, he says, they are committed to the 'liberal project' and they represent a moderate grouping within communitarianism who attempt to bridge 'the gap between a radical liberalism based on individual liberty, rights, and equality, and a radical conservatism rooted in tradition, duty and merit'.

Communitarian liberals attempt to offer a third way between the restrictive closed society implied by some communitarian thinkers and liberalism's open society, in which individuals exist within spheres of self-regarding immunity, between markets and hierarchy. Neither presents a realistic or workable model for modern society. What is needed is a balancing of the liberal interest in individual choice and autonomy with benefits accrued through one's duties and responsibilities to the community. Gray suggests that such a balance is a consequence of the recognition of the essentially social nature of individuals: 'the flourishing of individuals presupposes strong and deep forms of common life' (Gray 1996:16). Traditional liberalism has placed a great emphasis upon the autonomy and choice of the individual, and this has often been associated with an antipathy towards convention and social forces. For John Stuart Mill, for example, traditions and institutions were merely constraints upon individuality, and ought to be minimized as far as possible. This individuality, however, assumes the transmission of certain values from one generation to the next, and so presupposes a common culture of liberty and responsibility (Gray 1995b:55). It also assumes a powerful network of roles, institutions and obligations between members of the community if an individual's autonomy is to be protected and valued.

For its very existence, individualism depends upon forms of common life and culture. Autonomy, the condition in which persons can be at least part authors of their lives, will only have value if it is exercised in a community providing worthwhile options and supporting individual well-being. Therefore, it is the notion of a common culture that unites the apparently conflicting demands for duty and freedom as it lies at the heart of both. The understanding of community in terms of common culture offers a 'thinner' conception than that of many communitarian theorists. For reasons offered above, it is unlikely that we can ever recreate such a 'thick' community. It is important, though, to strengthen a form of community that is appropriate and viable in the modern world. This common culture must be reconciled to the fact that people are often members of a number of communities, and that in such a deeply pluralist society as modern Britain conflict between communities sometimes exists. Rather than playing down this diversity, it can be encouraged as a positive contribution to the life of the society, so long as it is supported by a framework of common culture. This common culture acts to facilitate the renewal and survival of those institutions that have been found to contribute to individual well-being and freedom (of the powerful?), while valuing a variety of practices that may lead to those goals. As such, Gray (1995b:57) believes they are merely the necessary elements of a civil society: toleration of others' views; a sense of responsibility for the welfare of others; equality before the law; and so on.

The role of the State in this communitarian liberal model is essentially one of umpire, maintaining the peace between conflicting groups and creating the structures necessary for an ongoing public conversation that generates a shared sense of fairness and reciprocity by ensuring that the values underpinning society are respected. The traditional liberal idea of State neutrality with regard to individual action is rejected in favour of a more positive contributory policy of actively developing the structures within the community necessary for its own continued existence. The most obvious of these structures is education, but they might also include policies to protect the weak and reintegrate the excluded members of the community. The communitarian liberal position is one that values both individual choice and action, but places it within the context of a rich and worthwhile common culture. As such, it seeks to avoid the pitfalls of excessive and illusory

individualism and conservatism. Fundamental to this view is the transmission of values and tradition's from one generation to the next, so
the institutions of the family and education take a paramount position,
without both of which the community would end.

New Labour and Communitarianism

Within the context of British politics, public philosophy communitarianism has had a major impact, particularly on the New Labour Party.
It is significant that when the Labour Party abandoned the 77-year-old
Clause Four of its Constitution in 1995 it replaced the clause with a
set of values that focused on community rather than economic intention (Tony Blair 1996:51–6). New Labour's aim became social
solidarity and community the chief means by which individuals could
flourish and develop. As Tony Blair was reported to say:

> We believe in the values of community, that by the strength of our
> commitment to common endeavour we can achieve the conditions
> in which individuals can realise their full potential. The basic prin-
> ciple is solidarity, that people can achieve much more by acting
> together than by acting alone. I think that all this is best repre-
> sented by the idea of community, in which each person has the
> rights and duties which go with community ... Rights are not
> enough. You can't build a society that isn't based on duty and
> responsibility.
>
> (*Guardian*, 13 March 1995)

The language is unmistakably communitarian in origin and appears
to be an American version of it. It aims to reconstruct the idea of the
home, school and the neighbourhood community within the context of
managed capitalism. The New Labour Party does not call it communitarian, preferring instead the even more ambiguous term, 'The Third
Way', which seems to be a route midway between the traditional
British Welfare State and the more individualistic welfare model of the
USA. It is therefore nothing but astonishing that this US inspired
public philosophy of communitarianism has displaced the much longer
political tradition of the Left in Britain. It is also difficult to see how
this new public philosophy links in with the Scottish and Christian
Socialist tradition of which Blair claims to be part, which strongly
emphasizes the ethical basis of community. Indeed, the work of the
Scottish moral philosopher, John MacMurray, one of Blair's intellectual

mentors, seems to have foreshadowed communitarianism in his ethical socialism (MacMurray 1992).

Even before Blair entered Parliament he was emphasizing community as his central theme, and at the 1991 Labour Party Conference he declared that individuals are not 'stranded in helpless isolation, but human beings, part of a community with obligations to one another'. His language increasingly adopted a distinct communitarian tone, but also built on the Christian socialism of the then party leader, John Smith, who advocated 'fellowship' and the belief that freedom was only meaningful and achievable within society. As Smith said, 'the combination of freedom and fellowship resulted in the obligation of service; service to family, to community and to nation' (quoted in John Rentoul 1995:295). Smith's ideas were derived not from public philosophy communitarianism, but from Christianity, while Blair increasingly turned his Christian socialism towards a more pronounced public philosophy communitarianism. Blair's notion of socialism was simply the principle that people can achieve more together than alone. This understanding appeared to ignore the content of socialism itself. His idea of community was also simply put as a moral entity in which people supported each other: an understanding of community which was full of sentimentality and nostalgia, but one which nevertheless attracted voters. As Shadow Home Secretary, Blair's communitarianism became even more developed in his speeches, especially when he said:

The break up of family and community bonds is intimately linked to the breakdown of law and order. Both family and community rely on notions of mutual respect and duty. It is in the family that we first learn to negotiate the boundaries of acceptable conduct and to recognise that we owe responsibilities to others as well as ourselves. We then build out from that family base to the community and beyond it to society as a whole. The values of a decent society are in many ways the values of the family unit, which is why helping to re-establish good family and community life should be a central objective of government policy, and that cannot be done without policies, especially in respect of employment and education, that improve society as a whole. We do not show our children respect or act responsibly to them if we fail to provide them with the opportunities they need, with a stake in the society in which they live. Equally, we demand that respect and responsibility from them in return.

(quoted in John Rentoul 1995:373–4)

This speech could have been written and delivered by Etzioni or any one of the American public philosophy communitarians. In the speech Blair was advocating one of the central communitarian principles – the superiority of common endeavour over individualism for sustaining the responsible community. The problem that New Labour face is how this communitarian idea of community can be translated into practical policies for the family and education service.

Beatrix Campbell (1995) believes that 'communitarianism' has prospered under New Labour. A number of the Party's young advisors have spent time in the USA studying communitarian ideas. However, Campbell comments harshly on New Labour's adoption of communitarianism:

> communitarianism is a *contingent* politics; it is associated with a political project that is both *abject* and *authoritarian*; it is dependent not on radicalism, on a culture of challenge fertilised by the conflict and solidarities of a popular culture, but on the traditionalism reinstated by the very same Thatcherism it purports to oppose.

Stephen Driver and Luke Martell (1997) also claim to detect a strong paternalistic current in New Labour and conclude that New Labour: 'increasingly favour conditional, morally prescriptive, conservative and individual communitarianisms. This is at the expense of less conditional and redistributional socio-economic progressive and corporate communitarianisms'. In other words, New Labour has moved from socialism and social democracy to a liberal conservatism 'which celebrates the dynamic market economy and is socially conservative'. It is why New Labour places emphasis on collective action in the community and blames the family, the individual and the relativist ethos for any social breakdown. New Labour has embraced communitarianism, but it is not clear with what communitarianism the Party is operating.

While Tony Blair has placed strong emphasis on 'community' as the central theme for New Labour, his own private decisions have been severely criticized for apparently undermining this newly adopted communitarian theme. In sending his son to the London Oratory School some felt, without the full reasons why he and his wife selected the London Oratory School, that Tony Blair had to readdress what he meant by 'community'. The London Oratory School was not part of the Blairs' *local* community. In an article for the *New Statesman* on 28 April

1995 Tony Blair wrote: 'The notion of community for me is less a geographical concept than a belief in the social nature of human beings'. Many of Blair's critics believed that this had reduced the meaning of community to vapid generality for they claimed that he was simply exercising the opportunities that excessive individualism had afforded him, while preaching a moral socialism which demanded that people support their local communities. Like the thinking of many other public philosophy communitarians Tony Blair, and New Labour with him, has adopted a pragmatic and flexible kind of communitarianism. Blair (1998:4) does not feel that this is an unprincipled position, indeed he says that 'a large measure of pragmaticism is essential' and that 'what matters is what works to give effect to our values'. New Labour has also given a high priority to education as the solution to unemployment and a renewed focus on technical education for employability which expresses a strong utilitarian strand in New Labour's thinking. Here Blair (1998:17) believes that a 'new pragmaticism is growing in the relations between the public and private sectors'. In an article in *The Times* on 6 July 1997 Tony Blair went so far as to write: 'Our children will learn more and earn more'.

Conclusion

The discussion of communitarianism in the succeeding chapters will show that many of its assumptions are rooted in classical (Aristotle) and medieval (Thomas Aquinas) philosophies which are interwoven with contemporary thought to make them more acceptable to a modern audience. Communitarian ideas are also connected with the development of the thought of Hegel who argued that no individual exists independently of other individuals within a society, and that personal identity is the result of a dialectical interplay between and among several individuals. Communitarianism is clearly in an evolving stage, both in theory and practice. Public philosophy communitarians are effectively conducting a straight-forwardly prescriptivist political argument within the public domain: they argue that human life will be better if common values guide and construct our lives. The appeal of 'common values' and 'community' are obvious, but they mean different things both to different people and to different political interests. The rise of communitarianism may be regarded as a positive development in that it marks a wider recognition of the inadequacies of the modern liberal approach to education. Communitarianism has helped push moral values and virtues to the centre stage in England

and Wales. It is concerned with the self-centred and excessive individualism that undermines the commitment to something beyond the self, let alone the public good and common traditions. However, there appears to be a growing number of positions taken up by people who call themselves communitarians and there is also growing criticism of the position itself. The term is not univocal and many are reluctant to own the expression. Liberal commentators in particular feel that they have not asserted individual autonomy against other people, but rather with other people. They claim that like the communitarian view they also seek to build around principles of cooperation and mutuality.

Communitarianism could be seen as a midway position between socialism and capitalism, but it espouses a rhetoric of moral education based on a secular morality that is not exactly clear. So when some call for communitarians to engage with other communities and voluntary organizations to create a common ground to deal with common problems, we are not exactly sure what is meant. This is especially the case when Etzioni (1997:257) states that the community should provide a moral framework, but that it is not the ultimate moral arbiter – this remains with the individual. In what ways, then, does he differ from liberalism? His new golden rule appears rather simplistic, since it has nothing to say about the specific choices, nor does it endorse particular moral principles, virtues or ideals. There is obviously a concern here in communitarian thought for social justice including minority rights, but the working out of these principles remains sketchy. Therefore, we can question whether or not communitarianism represents a satisfactory alternative to liberal individualism. There has been little in the way of a distinct and coherent public philosophy emerging from New Labour.

Some believe that communitarianism is a corrective to the excesses of liberalism, while others adopt the view that it is a source of reform for liberalism, and yet others still view it as an altogether distinctive approach to political theory. The philosophy is not an immediate blueprint for society's problems and it provides an inadequate analysis of social policy and economic conditions. This is why we need to be extremely cautious of the Communitarian Movement represented by Etzioni and his followers. There is also no explicit communitarian agenda for education in England and Wales other than some principles to guide the search for the moral values that should shape democratic society and communities. This may manifest itself in the continuation of the work of the long-established British community education movement which contains within it many of the principles of communitarianism.

With the communitarian emphasis on family values, some critics believe it could be a backward looking movement, both in scope and intention. It would appear to share much of the political conservatism of Edmund Burke (1729–1797) who believed that society was held together not by self-interest but by the feeling that we are members one of another. This conservative strain in communitarian thinking is well illustrated by Robert Nisbet's book *The Quest for Community*, first published in 1953, and in which he wrote:

> The family, religious association, and local community – these, the conservatives insisted, cannot be regarded as the external products of man's thought and behaviour; they are essentially prior to the individual and are the indispensable support of belief and conduct. Release man from the contexts of community and you get not freedom and rights but intolerable aloneness and subjection to demoniac fears and passions. Society, Burke wrote in a celebrated line, is a partnership of the dead, the living and the unborn. Mutilate the roots of society and tradition, and the result must inevitably be the isolation of a generation from its heritage, the isolation of individuals from their fellow men, and the creation of the sprawling, faceless masses.

Nisbet was concerned with the problem of community lost and community regained. However, he highlights the connection between conservatism and community and consequently the conservative communitarian longing for a sense of continuity and direction. While communitarians believe that a renewed sense of community will restore meaning and moral imperatives to individual lives, it appears that it is only acceptable to them as long as the notion of community remains vague. Another weakness in communitarian theory is that it could be seen to justify the silencing of individuals in favour of a rhetorical appeal to community, solidarity and shared values. As Etzioni said himself, in the journal *The Responsive Society: Rights and Responsibilities* (1991:149–50): 'While the concept of community may harbour the threat of coercion, it is not the coercion of the state, but the moral compulsion of a Salem-like community'.

At the policy level, John Marenbon (1997) argues that New Labour's use of the rhetoric of communitarianism is merely an excuse to expand government and threaten individual autonomy. Certainly, communitarianism challenges liberal rationalism by attempting to restore the balance between diversity and unity, critical thought and shared traditions and between autonomy and community. However, it is doubtful whether it has really succeeded in supplying us with a coherent, intellectually sound, and compelling alternative to the dominant liberal model. In many respects communitarianism appears to be about saving liberalism from itself while at the same time it is a reaction to both social liberal and conservative (libertarian) perspectives. Although it may appear that there is no viable alternative to liberalism, the following chapters explore a number of issues related to the community–individual nexus as it relates to families and schools. The discussion of communitarianism in this chapter has implications for the aims and purposes of schooling, and will be of growing significance if present and future United Kingdom governments begin to embrace policies derived from aspects of communitarian theory. Of all the policies and debates originating within the communitarian perspective, perhaps the most influential and immediate in the public arena are those concerning the family. It is important at this stage to review both the perceived and actual changes which have contributed to the current debate on the family.

2 Communitarianism and the Family

The dear, dreamy old bachelor notion – that notion that the unity of marriage, the being one flesh, has something to do with being perfectly happy, or being perfectly good, or even being perfectly and continuously affectionate! I tell you, an ordinary honest man is a part of his wife even when he wishes he wasn't. I tell you, an ordinary good women is part of her husband even when she wishes him at the bottom of the sea. I tell you that, whether the two people are for the moment friendly or angry, happy or unhappy, the Thing marches on, the great four-footed Thing, the quadruped of the home. They are a nation, a society, a machine. I tell you they are one flesh, even when they are not one spirit.

(G. K. Chesterton, quoted in Maisie Ward's, *Return to Chesterton* 1952)

This decade has witnessed a continuation of changes in the structure and status of the family which seem to have been accelerated in the late 1960s and early 1970s. While the traditional family, in which a mother and father marry, have children who live with both parents until they grow up and begin their own adult lives, is still the most common form of family structure in Britain (Kathleen Kiernan 1998:51), many conservative thinkers and religious groups have expressed their concern that this situation may not last. Conservative thinkers continue to blame feminism, secularism and over-dependency on the Welfare State for what they see as the decline of the family. As Jon Davies (1993:95) put it: 'In all probability the "normal" marriage and family life are headed for the history books'. This may or may not be the case (the suspicion is that it is not). Liberals often focus on the economic causes for the changes in family life, especially what they claim to be inadequate welfare support. Some progressive thinkers go further, which has resulted in a great deal of writing and commentary in education, ethics and the social sciences being taken up with statements that amount to the claim that the traditional family's position of pre-eminence, as the 'ideal' form, is indefensible. Family life, some commentators hold, is not deteriorating, but simply changing (Norman Dennis and George Erdos 1993), and this is an inevitable consequence of changing wider social and economic structures. These commentators refuse to say whether or not these changes are for the better. This chapter examines the changing face of family life in Britain as part of Western society. It outlines some of the most significant aspects of the debate on family structure that have led theorists and politicians, most notably the communitarians, to articulate policy proposals. One vital element of the discussion that lies at the centre of the communitarian agenda for the family is the moral development of young children within the family, which is also explored in this chapter.

The Communitarians and the Family

The family lies at the heart of a great deal of communitarian thinking. This is a predictable consequence of communitarian views of the make-up of society, in which society is constituted by a network of increasingly smaller and closer-knit groups, through which it is joined to the individual. Inherent within communitarian perspectives is the assumption that it is these groups, these communities, that offer society its shape, character and value. Of course, it is not at communities that this process ends. A further level is needed, by which the community acquires its shape, character and values, or as John O'Neill (1994:4) says: 'Families make communities; communities make states'. Also, insofar as the family is a collection of individuals, it offers a model for living within the wider community; it is the 'first community' (Norton Garfinkle 1998:10). At each point, the family represents a community and membership of the family can, potentially, act as a form of social template for membership of the wider community. Likewise, as membership of a community, according to the majority of communitarianisms, implies interdependencies that impose non-voluntary moral obligations to others, so family membership involves a series of responsibilities and a relationship of reciprocity without which the family could not function. As John Gray (1993:52) says: 'We are born in families, encumbered without our consent by obligations we cannot by voluntary choice renounce'.

A number of recent communitarian writers have developed this emphasis, as well as supplementing it with concrete policy proposals. For Etzioni, for example, the family is at the core of the 'moral infrastructure' (Etzioni 1997:176) necessary for the survival of communities. Critics have often characterized this position as conservative and even anachronistic (cf. Demaine and Entwhistle 1998). However, these communitarians have insisted that they are not trying to turn back the clock, and that they are endeavouring to offer a model of families within communities that is contemporary and relevant for modern society (Etzioni 1997:177, William Galston 1991:150). Henry Tam (1998) has claimed that communitarianism can be distinguished from alternative viewpoints in that it attempts to transcend the traditional/progressive divide by addressing contemporary issues in a constructive, balanced manner: 'Against both the authoritarian and individualist positions, communitarians target its criticisms, not at old or new forms of structures as such, but at parental behaviour which undermines the needs of children' (ibid.:72).

Whether or not they have an orientation towards traditional structures, a great many of the communitarians' statements regarding the family are aligned explicitly with the two-parent model (cf. Galston 1991, Etzioni 1997, 1993, Gray 1993). In response to criticisms, they might argue that their advocacy of any particular family structure is not derived from a view of it as somehow sacred, but rather from the conviction that it is 'the most effective answer' (Etzioni 1997:180) to everyday problems of social existence and parenthood. Or, as Henry Tam (1998:72) puts it: 'What citizens should praise or blame is not particular family patterns, but the extent to which their fellow citizens carry out their responsibilities as parents'. However, as Jeffrey Blustein (1982) has shown, this underlies almost all traditional justifications of family form. Communitarian positions on the family are generally made up of a series of related premises, beginning with the assertion of the essential moral nature of the parental role: 'Making a child is a moral act' (Etzioni 1993:54). The moral dimensions of parenting can be considered as a three-way relationship between children, their parents and the community. By virtue of their position, parents are duty-bound to protect and nurture their dependent children. In Blustein's (1982:116) phrasing, these are 'duties of need-fulfilment' grounded on a concern for the essential helplessness of young children.

For many communitarians, the moral aspect of parents' roles also extends outside the family, since the community as a whole lives with the consequences of their procreation: the whole community pays if a child grows up to be dependent upon welfare support; the whole community suffers if there is a lack of suitable members of society; the whole community suffers if society is unsafe and divided. A society's existence depends upon a substantial part of the population possessing shared virtues and attitudes. Since these communitarians take the family to be the origin of such virtues and attitudes, they hold that the community has a legitimate interest in promoting the formation and sustenance of stable and effective families (Galston 1991:145). In other words, the community in which a family lives is affected by the consequences, both positive and negative, of child-rearing, and, therefore, the community has both a right and an obligation to be involved in it. Therefore, it becomes incumbent upon parents to ensure that their children are educated and properly socialized into the community, possessing both the core values that allow them to live peaceably with others and the ability to contribute to the community through their work or efforts. Following a similar logic, a community must have a responsibility towards its families, mainly through assisting those families to carry out their parental duties as well as possible. The degree to which the community might be involved in supporting families could vary from a general ethos of support and interest to more specific interventions, such as ensuring reasonable tax levels, adequate work opportunities, reduced tension between work and home, and community-wide support services. Each of these would better place parents in their fundamental responsibility – that of bringing up children well. As Etzioni (1993:40) observes: 'A community that is more respectful of its children would make parenting a less taxing and more fulfilling experience'.

Parents might also claim an entitlement to a degree of freedom and autonomy in their dealings with their offspring, but, of course, their freedom is conditional upon them exercising it responsibly. Tam (1998) is most explicit regarding the implications of these conditions. The initial response to a family failing to carry out its duty in the rearing of its children is an educational one: parents unable to cope require training in the necessary skills. However, Tam is quite unequivocal that the proper preparation of children for later community life is so fundamental to his communitarian agenda, that parents who clearly fail to discharge their duties towards their children would risk losing those children (ibid.:73). In effect, he is arguing against the sovereign authority of parenthood and in favour of a community-based authority, in which parents are merely the deliverers of training, accountable to a higher court: 'People who have made no adequate preparation when they (intentionally or accidentally) have children should be required to make those preparations or their children will be adopted by people who have made appropriate preparations' (ibid.:75).

This sovereignty of community is most apparent when Tam discusses the problem of clashing goals, in which parents' views of education, for example, do not match those of the community. In such cases, he argues (ibid.:73), the community has the right (or the duty) to intercede on behalf of the child and insist that the appropriate values are adopted, since the inculcation of values is the most central of the community's duties to the child: ensuring preparation for a full and meaningful life. Fundamental to the community's duties to the child is the creation of a 'civil' environment conducive to his or her overall development and education. This may necessitate certain punitive measures to protect the young against vices and threats present in society. More important, however, are actions to support parents. As Ringen Stein (1998:12) correctly argues, the raising of children is a job that families carry out for society, and as such there is a common interest to ensure that they succeed. This can happen in a number of ways: through the support of grandparents, friends and the wider family, through neighbours and through community organizations. These groups can offer emotional and instrumental support (information and advice on child-care, for example), as well as reinforcing moral and social expectations, so that the child receives consistent messages regarding appropriate behaviour and standards.

It would seem that there is another dimension necessary to complete a communitarian perspective, although it is not one that has been articulated by the writers under review. In this perspective, the child, too, has duties to its parents and the wider community. The communitarians frequently claim to be in favour of a balance of rights and responsibilities, and there is no obvious reason why this ought not extend to children. There are, broadly speaking, two type of duties of relevance to the present discussion. Children have a temporary duty to their parents and those acting *in loco parentis*, to cooperate with their demands (assuming that those demands are reasonable and fair). Thomas Aquinas referred to this as duty of obedience, in which juniors suppress their will in favour of the will of more experienced or otherwise superior others. Children also have a permanent duty to others through their continual reliance upon their support and care. Parents, 'the closest source of our existence and development' (Aquinas, 1991 translation, qu. 101, article 1), effect such benefits to their children over the course of their lives that it is incumbent upon their children to respond to them in a special way, through respect and through actual assistance when they need it – for example, in later life when they may need care and support (Blustein 1982:162–95).

Most communitarians who have written on the family have tended to adopt William Galston's stance, that: 'It is time, I suggest, to put the family at the center of our thinking about social policy, and children at the center of our thinking about the family' (1991:145). In other words, they have approached the thorny question of family structure from the perspective of the needs of the child. Almost every major modern communitarian writer has concluded that a two-parent family, in the traditional mould, is the most appropriate model for children's overall development (for example, cf. Etzioni 1997:180, Galston 1991:150).

They tend to justify this position on surprisingly pragmatic grounds: bringing up children is a taxing, time-consuming job, requiring almost constant effort, communication and engagement; it is made easier if the load is shared by two people with similar values and a shared commitment to remain with their children. There is nothing in this equation that leads one to justify the inequalities inherent in many traditional families; on the contrary, Etzioni (1998) goes so far as to offer a new twist on the two-parent family, the 'peer marriage', in which 'both father and mother have the same rights and the same responsibilities' (ibid.:180). Moreover, advocacy of the two-parent family does not mean that it is always the best option; it is conceivable that in some situations a single parent will be the best solution to a particular set of problems. Nonetheless, at the level of society-wide phenomena, most communitarians claim that significant differences in outcomes of patterns of child-rearing do occur and should be enshrined in a general social policy. William Galston (1991), who is a good representative of this communitarian position, argues that the law and public policy cannot and should not be neutral among ends and should therefore foster in its citizens the virtues consistent with the social good. It is why he believes that the single-parent family is a largely unsatisfactory arrangement for the rearing of children. Iris Young (1994) disputes Galston's arguments from a liberal feminist position by counter-arguing that it is wrong for government to encourage particular family forms and discourage others. Young is concerned to protect the freedom of women as equal and respected citizens to raise children themselves, independently of any dependency on men, if they so choose. She therefore says (1994:130): 'Public policy should promote and encourage the ends and purposes of families. Contrary to what Galston argues, however, public policy should not *prefer* particular means of realizing these ends'.

Liberals tend to affirm a plurality of family forms as valid ways of life. However, the emerging British public policy on the family under New Labour, that some would describe as family values rhetoric, seems to *prefer* particular means over others and is much closer to Galston's communitarian position.

UK Politics and the Family

All major political parties and positions in the United Kingdom have offered some support for a communitarian perspective on the family (Willets 1994, Young and Halsey 1995, Gray 1996). Alongside a general support for the importance of community within modern society, the value that communitarians place on the family has struck a chord with much recent discussion in the political world. The Conservative government of Margaret Thatcher readily identified itself as the 'Party of the Family'. This statement summarizes the inherent difficulty within the Conservative Party's family stance, which was a combination of liberal (and at times libertarian) valuing of the individual's rights and dominion in public affairs against a more general conservative emphasis upon traditional family structures. Her replacement as Tory leader and Prime Minister, John Major, maintained an emphasis upon the family: the 'Back to Basics' campaign was unambiguously supportive of the traditional two-parent family. However, a great deal of the legislation brought about during the Conservative government also pushed towards greater individual rights. The Family Law Act (1996), the Children Act (1989) and similar legislation seems to have resulted in liberalization of the family and its members by the removal of existing barriers to divorce, giving married women greater access to their husbands' property, and giving children greater rights, all of which has led Rob Killick (1996:8) to argue that: 'It may not be too much of an exaggeration to argue that [Conservative] family policy has been more influenced by feminist campaigns of the seventies than the moral right!'

The 'New Labour' Government of Tony Blair maintained the emphasis upon the family within social policy, with its very first policy document focusing upon the relationship between schools and families. More overtly acknowledging a communitarian perspective than previous UK governments, Blair's administration has increasingly advocated a combination of punishment and partnership with respect to families. It has stressed the need for parents to cooperate with the State in raising educational standards and reducing youth crime. For example, the Secretary of State for Education, David Blunkett, also referred to the role of the family in the foreword to *Excellence in Schools*:

> Excellence can only be achieved on the basis of partnership. We all need to be involved: schools, teachers and parents are at the heart of it. We also need the help of all of you: families and the wider community.
>
> (DfE 1997: cm 368:3)

The government has advocated punitive measures for those families and individuals who fail to fulfil their obligations to their offspring and the wider community, such as threats to cut welfare support for single mothers. Home Secretary Jack Straw has embraced a number of the proposals of the communitarians, and his approach to family policy involves such schemes as parenting classes, curfews for children, early relationship groups and toddler training groups, to name but a few of the many proposals being raised from government sources. The New Labour government produced a consultation paper, *Supporting Families* (Home Office 1998) which represents its first family policy paper. There is some confusion in the document in that the government explicitly says that marriage is the best unit in which to bring up children, but immediately asserts that lone parents and unmarried couples are also successfully rearing children. The consultation document envisages the creation of a National Family and Parenting Institute based on similar organizations in Australia, Austria and Canada, which provide advice to government on family policy and offer practical support measures for families themselves. The government propose a huge range of issues and statements for public discussion, some of which have a heavily moral tone; those issues and statements directly concerned with education can be listed as:

- Parents educate us, and they teach right from wrong (p. 4);
- Good parents improve a child's schooling (p. 6);
- Parents should be helped to help their children through family literacy schemes to be developed through a new Family Literacy Initiative (pp. 6 and 16);
- Education for parenthood should be part of the school curriculum and all children should be taught the responsibility of parenthood (pp. 6 and 17);
- Parents should be helped with school liaison (p. 7);

- The establishment of 'school-settling groups' should help parents with control and discipline and how to cooperate with teachers on the standards and behaviour that can be expected from their children (p. 13);
- Parents must know their responsibilities to ensure that their children attend school and behave properly (p. 15);
- Partnership between schools and parents at all stages is the key to raising educational attainment (p. 16);
- Parents need to support schools in dealing with children who do not attend school on a regular basis (p. 16);
- Schools should look at ways to involve a child's grandparents in school (p. 18);
- An Education Maintenance Allowance should be established to help young people over 16 years of age to remain in full-time study (p.23);
- There should be home–school agreements in all schools that explain the responsibilities of both the school and parents and which parents should sign (p. 41);
- Parents should have access to an independent parental supporter when their children need special educational needs in school (p. 42);
- Schools should raise the awareness of domestic violence in the home and promote tolerance and peaceful resolution (p. 46).

Few of these proposals are new and many schools already implement and offer a range of these measures in order to build and strengthen their partnerships with parents. Moreover, the government is already seeking the widespread adoption of some of these practices by presenting them as examples of good practice before any national discussion has begun of the consultation paper. Critics argue that it is merely a government attempt at building morality through a policy of intervention in the family, which in turn undermines the moral authority of parents. Others claim it is an artificial attempt by the State to introduce morality because the State can claim no moral authority. Perhaps a more accurate interpretation would be to say that the government has adopted a pragmatic, largely utilitarian approach to the family in the hope of supporting the political and social structures of society.

Changes to Family Structure

Undoubtedly, there have been enormous changes in the patterns of lifestyle in the Western world during the last few decades, and some would argue that these outstrip any other reforms that have taken place in the structuring of the family since early Christian thinkers such as Augustine and Aquinas set out to prescribe the characteristics of a 'good' family. On the other hand, as we have seen, the intact two-parent family remains the norm, despite reports of its demise. At the same time, however, a variety of 'alternative' family lifestyles have emerged that compete with the traditional model: single mothers; single fathers; co-habitees. Indeed, some have gone so far to say that these new forms of the family are not just as good, but often better than the traditional husband and wife team. These developments have taken place quite rapidly, and it is worth considering the reasons for their emergence, to help evaluate what critics see as the decline in parental culture.

Norman Dennis and George Erdos (1993) trace the origins of the overt challenge to the traditional marriage to the early 1970s, when a host of social and economic changes coincided. Before that time, they claim that child-rearing and life-long mutual aid had far greater importance than sexual pleasure, grounded, as they were, upon an implicitly religious notion of the sanctity of marriage and procreation. For a number of reasons, they continue, this situation began to lose its appeal, and its place was increasingly taken by rational exchange (ibid.:60), whereby individual self-interest came to guide the starting, ending and nature of relationships. Attitudes towards sex, which were once traditionally rooted in religious dogma, became located in the private domain, and this was related to the advent of modern contraception and abortion procedures. A growing individualism and an associated rights-based philosophy began to offer increasing influence over the middle classes, in the first instance, and subsequently large elements of the wider society. Dennis and Erdos do not offer a full historical account of the changes to marriage and parenting, but appear instead to focus and begin their commentary from the 1960s, as do many contemporary writers on the subject. This inevitably weakens their arguments, no matter how much they may appeal, as modern explanations for the decline of marriage. One conservative commentator, Melanie Phillips (1996:233), an admirer of some of the new communitarians, has been encouraged by such arguments to say that:

> The concept of parenting has been diminished by the me-society. The very idea of duty has been replaced by rights: the right of a child to assent itself against the authority of adults; the right of adults to live as they please regardless of the consequences.

Unfortunately, her approach is both overtly journalistic and sensationalist and she adopts only those elements within communitarian thinking that lend support to her conservative beliefs and rhetoric of society's moral decay.

These changes in the social world reflected reforms in education and social policy. The Plowden Report of 1967, for example, signalled a movement towards child-centred teaching methods and a greater recognition of the interests of the child in determining curriculum content. There was also a parallel growth of interest in developmental psychology. The work of Piaget, for example, was continually misused and misapplied, with a resultant unwillingness on the part of some parents and educators to force the child in any learning situation, but rather to wait until the child was 'ready'. To a lesser extent, such crude and inaccurate views persist, as can be seen from this guidance on how to react when discovering your child has stolen, offered by Penelope Leach (1989:461, emphasis added), one of the most influential writers in child-care:

> Obviously you want to be careful that your child does not appear to steal, because other people are likely to make such a song and dance about it. But *don't make it a moral issue at this stage.*

Perhaps the most influential change in political consciousness, as it relates to the family, was that of the democratization and equalization of family roles – at least at the level of rhetoric, since in reality this has not always happened. On the one hand, adults insisted that their rights to freedom from the chains of parenthood deserved acknowledgement, and on the other, some children's rights campaigners claimed similar liberty and autonomy for children. An example of the latter view is the well-known writer, John Holt (1975), who argued that a truly equal society would be one in which children would be able to vote, and choose their parents! Many of the obvious changes in family structure and status which have become common in recent years can be traced to the later 1960s and early 1970s, but the reasons for these changes are both more complex and began before the 1960s. By examining statistical data on family structure from the 1970s we find a significant and unprecedented demographic change occurred. Drawing upon the surveys by John Haskey (1998) and Dennis and Erdos (1993) and United Kingdom government statistics it is possible to provide an overview of these changes, some of which are outlined below:

- women are having fewer children, are child-bearing at a later age, and are increasingly childless;
- family sizes are reducing;
- there has been a decline in extended families;
- there has been a growth in living alone;
- there has been an increase in lone-motherhood in never-married women (8 per cent in 1971 – 19 per cent in 1991, General Household Survey 22, 1993);
- there has been an increase in conceptions and births outside marriage (conceptions – 21 per cent in 1971 – 43 per cent in 1990; births – 9 per cent in 1976 – 34 per cent in 1995, Social Trends 23, 1993), and a consequent growth in co-habiting couples and lone-motherhood (by 1990/1 7 per cent of 16–24 year old men and 12 per cent of 25–34 year old men were cohabiting outside marriage, General Household Survey 22, 1993);
- there has been a growth in divorce;
- there has been an increase in married couple step-families.

To summarize his survey, John Haskey (1998:32–3) writes: 'family and household structures have never been more diverse … Individuals are more likely to experience living in a greater variety of types of families and households during their lifetime'.

Considerable structural changes have taken place during the last two decades related to family and parenthood. The economic turbulence and the effect of Thatcherite policies during the Conservative governments between 1979 and 1997 certainly had a negative influence on the family that may well have been greater than the generally liberal influences from the 1960s. This in itself need not be of significance to those concerned with public policy like some communitarians, since their concerns may focus more upon the moral and social development of children. So long as children's well-being and their ability to play constructive roles in society are not harmed by the changes, there would be no need to interfere. Many communitarian theorists do claim, however, that there can be negative consequences arising out of certain of the changes in family structure, and that these need to be identified and addressed.

Patterns seem to be emerging from the tentative research on family, and the message is not one that communitarians would generally welcome. A range of studies in the field suggest that certain non-traditional family structures are associated with harmful outcomes for children in those families. The family, many communitarians suggest, is the microcosm in which children first observe, acquire and exhibit the values and pro-social behaviour necessary for successful integration into the wider community. In part, the child's initiation is brought about by conscious effort on the part of the parents and other carers, by reinforcing accept-able behaviour and punishing or challenging unacceptable behaviour. However, the structural aspects of the child's social environment also play a vital role. The two-parent family ideally involves a complex web of negotiations between the parents: it involves, with various degrees of success, communication and compromise, reciprocity and coopera-tion. This exists alongside any moral education that parents might intend to carry out. In this respect, the medium really is the message as Miriam David (1998:69) says:

> Unless a child is brought up in the constant atmosphere of human beings negotiating the business of getting on with one another, co-operating, controlling their anger, effecting reconciliations, he cannot learn what it is to be an effective member of a society group.

If this is the case, changes to a family's structure would seem likely to result in changes to social learning in that family's children. More specifically, the deterioration (or non-existence) of the inherent need to negotiate and cooperate might adversely affect the children's learning of a host of pro-social skills and behaviours. A number of research projects suggest that changes in patterns of parenting are, indeed, becoming associated with increasing social problems among children and young people, including delinquency and social exclusion, impov-erished personal relationships and reduced educational achievement (cf. Garfinkle 1998, Bright 1997).

The Family and Moral Development

There is enormous theoretical and empirical support for the common-sense idea that early years experiences are a central factor in later social and moral development (Norton Garfinkle 1998, Robert Coles 1997, Rosamund Miles 1994, William Damon, 1988), and the family is the main source of such learning. For example, it is through the family that a young child learns values and society's norms, its emotional needs are met, its identity begins to develop, all underpinned by a sense of security upon which these other elements of normal develop-ment are built. A number of communitarian thinkers have drawn upon this view to support their broader notion of a secure and settled community into which the child becomes initiated. Of particular significance is the notion of 'attachment', which Norton Garfinkle (1998:3) has claimed is the central conception in all early years research into cognitive and moral development. Communitarians argue, with support from psychological literature, that the quality of the attachment between children and their parents formed in the first years of life, is a powerful indicator of later well-being. Conversely, children denied the opportunity of establishing strong bonds with parents, or perhaps other carers, appear to be at much great risk of suffering in terms of their psychological and cognitive development. Rosenblith and Knight (1989) list a number of characteristics associated with well-attached infants (as opposed to their less securely attached peers), which include greater cooperation when working with both adults and peers, more likelihood to lead in activities, willingness to ask adults for assistance, greater curiosity and a greater capacity to deal with adversity and problems. Each of these qualities can contribute to the growing child's ability to deal with others and with the day-to-day challenges of everyday life. At the same time, the caring, supportive relationships necessary for such attachment act as the young child's first experiences of interacting with other people, and lead to certain expectations about relationships outside the family. The parents, after all, are also the child's first authority figures and the first models of behaviour. It is in the family, therefore, that the child receives the first lessons in social roles, reciprocity and responsibility.

Franz et al. (cited in David Popenoe 1994) in a longitudinal study, taking place over 36 years, found that the dimension most closely correlated to social accomplishment in adulthood was a warm and affectionate mother or father. David Popenoe (1994), however, has argued that attachment alone is insufficient and that, as well as supporting and nurturing, parents also need to prohibit and limit certain actions, and teach and reinforce certain values and behaviours. This relates closely to the pioneering research of Diane Baumrind (1973, 1989, cf. William Damon 1988) into parenting styles. She found that many effective parents exhibited a combination of warmth, communication and high control. Less effective patterns could often be characterized as either permissive or authoritarian. The former was associated with a warm and caring environment, but without sufficient rules and controls for children to develop an internalized means of controlling their behaviour. The latter, while strong on control, lacked the communication between parents and children, and often resulted in children lacking an understanding of the 'reasons' for rules.

Diane Baumrind advocated a third parenting model, which she labelled 'authoritative' (although she accepted that this was not the only means of rearing happy, socially responsible children). The authoritative approach is a combination of high control, clear communication and warmth. Rules and standards of behaviour are directly addressed by the parent, but in an environment of what William Damon (1988:119) labelled 'respectful engagement'. In this way, the adult does not abdicate his or her responsibility to guidance, but also attempts to build a bridge between these standards and the child's inclinations. Communication, according to Baumrind's research, is vital if children are to develop a sense of personal responsibility, and the behaviour necessary to become active members of their community: 'Friendly rather than hostile to peers, facilitative rather than disruptive of others' work, and co-operative rather than resistive of adult-led activity' (Baumrind 1973). Much recent debate in education and child development has centred on the question of whether it is preferable to develop children's values through the reinforcement of certain character traits or habits (as seems to be the theme of the US Character Education movement; cf. Brooks and Goble 1997, Thomas Likona 1991) or through a process of reflection about moral issues (which lies at the heart of the highly influential Values Clarification philosophy, Louis Raths et al. 1966). To a certain extent, this distinction relates to the traditional conservative/liberal debate in education, centring upon the question of whether it is most appropriate to foster the 'habits' necessary to fit into the existing society or to encourage reflection upon those values.

William Damon (1995) has argued that this is a false distinction, since both good habits and reflection are necessary aspects of the moral life, particularly in a modern, liberal society. Habits of good conduct, bolstered through years of reinforcement and practice, are the foundations upon which the moral life is built, since they guide the majority of moral behaviour. Clearly, it would be unworkable for children (and adults) to meditate upon every choice presented to them, and social living assumes that many habits are internalized by the child at a relatively early age. There are, times, however, when these habitual patterns of behaviour fall short, perhaps due to unexpected conditions or circumstances. In these cases, it is important for the child to be able to understand the community's values and their implications, in order to act in an appropriate way. Consequently, through experience and variety, under the guidance of caring, supportive parents and other adults, the child learns to integrate these elements into patterns of moral behaviour. As William Damon (1995:158) concludes: 'Reflection grounded in good values, supports rather than deflects the habitual moral response ... Only when habit and reflection marry does sustained moral commitment become possible'.

Travis Hirschi's (1969) theory of delinquency and control offers a valuable insight into the importance of a child's early experiences within the family, specifically as it relates to the adoption of or resistance to delinquent behaviour. He suggested that in terms of crime and delinquency, the important question was not 'Why do children commit crimes?' but rather 'Why don't they?' In other words, Travis Hirschi sought to identify those factors that led to compliance with social norms and standards of behaviour. His model hypothesized a number of elements in a child's life necessary for the avoidance of criminal behaviour, including attachment to significant others (including adults at school and peers), involvement in community activities and belief in the moral validity of society's rules. Hirschi gave precedence, however, to the role played by parents in the child's development. Conformity, he argued, was the result of a bond (which relates closely to the previous conception of 'attachment'), and as the bond weakens, so does the probability increase of an child becoming involved in anti-social behaviour, and the first and most important bond is with family. People internalize social norms and values because they are concerned about the response of their kin, and Hirschi (1969:88) says: 'The important consideration is whether the parent is psychologically present when temptation to commit crime appears'. Children who are strongly attached to their parents will know that misbehaviour will be a source of distress to them, and consequently try to avoid deviance. Attachment to a parent or parents, therefore, acts as a primary deterrent to children's engagement in delinquency, and the force of this attachment depends upon the time and quality of parent–child interactions and relationships.

According to this theory, close parental supervision, intimate communication and affectionate relationships form the basis of pro-social development in children. Conversely, the theory predicts that absence of these qualities would be positively associated with an increased probability of delinquency, and this does seem to be the case, as has been seen, for example in the studies cited by West (1994) following 411 London boys from childhood to adulthood. Likewise, recent Home Office research identifies low parental supervision and conflict in the home as among the strongest risk factors that relate to young people starting to offend (Graham and Bowling 1995). None of the above suggests a necessary relationship between family structure and crime.

Almost any form of family can provide the warmth and support so fundamental for growth and development. The central factor leading to problems seems to be what Young and Halsey (1995) call 'time poverty', that is, too little time devoted by parents to their children. Clearly this can be a serious concern for single-parents, who often have to balance the range of time-consuming roles traditionally shared by two people. Moreover, the 'dense and continuous' (David 1998:69) interaction of adults necessary for the child to learn the cooperation underpinning social engagement is likely to be missing from a home in which there is only one regular adult present. On the other hand, the threat of time poverty exists for two-parent families as well, particularly in recent years, when both parents may be forced to work very soon after the child has been born.

There exists in any society a real danger that parents will not have enough time dedicated to their children, especially when they need it most. Although this danger cannot be attributable to a particular form of family life, many communitarians believe that the changes in the structure of family life are a cause for concern. A longitudinal study carried out as part of the National Child Development Study on children born in 1958 (Ferri 1993) found a number of patterns, including:

- children of broken marriages were more likely to finish school at the earliest opportunity and to leave home before eighteen years of age than children of surviving marriages;
- children of broken marriages were more likely to suffer from psychological problems;
- girls in step-families had twice the risk of pregnancy while teenagers;
- girls and boys in step-families were twice as likely to leave school at sixteen.

Similar findings, particularly as they relate to schooling, had been discovered by two seminal studies. Both the survey of James Coleman et al. (1987) and research by Michael Rutter et al. (1979) found that many of the seemingly vital factors in schooling, such as pupil–teacher ratios, library resources, expenditure on pupils, and so on had relatively little effect upon student educational achievement. A more significant variable seemed to be the less *objective* factor of family background, which James Coleman et al. (1987:13) identified as having a 'profound' effect upon educational achievement.

It is an extremely sensitive issue to study the contemporary family, and research can just as easily be used in a misleading way as a source of illumination. Nevertheless, it is too important a matter to be avoided, especially as it plays so central a role in the character of the community and the wider society. Therefore, from a communitarian perspective, an honest appraisal of the situation is essential. An American writer summarized the research findings on the relationship between family background and social achievement, thus:

> The social science evidence is in: though it may benefit the adults involved, the dissolution of intact two-parent families is harmful to large numbers of children. Moreover ... family diversity in the form of increase in numbers of single-parent and step-parent families does not strengthen the social fabric, but, rather, dramatically weakens and undermines society.
>
> (Barbara Whitehead, quoted in Dennis and Erdos 1993:xvi)

Once again, it should be remembered that these findings are not suggesting that it is impossible for single-parents or step-parents to bring up their children to be perfectly well-adjusted and active citizens. However, the research is based upon statistical aggregation, and identifies significant patterns. The consequence seems obvious: if the research findings to date are correct (and few have offered reasonable cases to question them), then the communitarians' insistence that a serious look at social policy as it relates to the family is necessary, indeed, urgent. If it is acknowledged that some of the changes in family structure are harmful to the children who experience it and to society as a whole, then a policy that is more protective of the young must be in order.

Conclusion

Until recently the phrase 'family values' was most often associated with conservative attempts at defending traditional concepts of family life. Today, the phrase is being addressed by conservatives and liberals alike, but the latter have shifted the debate from moral values to one of the well-being of children. New Labour, in particular, has adopted a pragmatic approach in social policy that recognizes that changes in the family have been costly to the economy and are potentially damaging to the welfare of children. The reasons for the expansion of different family forms are both complex and many, but among these reasons can be counted an increase in individualism, changing economic patterns, and psychological causes. Nevertheless, claims that the traditional family will very soon become a thing of the past seem inaccurate: the type and pace of change in recent years has been significant, but there is no evidence or reason to suggest that the traditional family will eventually cease to exist. Rather, the pattern seems to be the development of a range of family structures that society tolerates (and may even come to celebrate).

The two-parent family continues to be the norm, and the 'logic' of parent–child relationships discussed in this chapter might suggest that this continues to be the case, even though this form becomes located within an increasingly wide range of alternatives. The moral relativism at the heart of much of the writing in this field seems both dubious and potentially harmful to society in general and to young children in particular. In addition much of the available research points to the key notion that moral behaviour, reflection and autonomy develop slowly and gradually within stable, consistent and authoritative (but not authoritarian) environments, and that the most important of these, by far, is the parent–child relationship. Parenthood, rather than marriage, seems the key and it is grounded upon distinct moral bases (Blustein 1982), and it is a matter of empirical assessment whether the welfare of children is best met through the traditional married couple. The research findings are not as clear as traditionalists sometimes imply. What does seem clear, however, is that parents within a stable, loving relationship are the best environment for the moral and social development of children. The British government accepts that the most obvious, but certainly not the only source of this stability is the two-parent family.

Most communitarians feel no need to draw upon arguments for the intrinsic worth of the two-parent family. Rather, they argue that it is common sense to recognize that bringing up children is a costly affair, in terms of time, money and energy. Two parents are preferable to one (Etzioni 1993:60), but only if they are good at parenting. The duties of and demands upon parents are such that the task is made easier and less burdensome when the stress is taken by a number of people, each of whom has the child's interests at heart. One possible objection to the talk of duties and obligations of parents is that it is too dry and formal in representing the relationships between parents and their children. Of course, some of the most valuable aspects of any such relationship are the love and affection felt between members of a family, and many parents need not be reminded of their obligations. Duty, it may seem, might conflict with other elements of family life that arise spontaneously, but the fact remains that not all parents fulfil their obligations to their children at all times, whether due to ignorance, malice or indifference, and it is in these situations that talk of duties becomes relevant.

A sound social policy must be firmly grounded upon good reasons and evidence. New Labour have therefore sought a greater public discussion of the duties of parents and families in nurturing their children within society. In particular, New Labour has articulated the various ways in which parents can develop the full educational potential of their children in collaboration and partnership with teachers, schools and the wider community. There is also a recognition by the government that parents will need significant support in order to fulfil the duties of parenthood. In connection with the parental partnership with schools the government's view could be summarized in Thomas Likona's words (1991:35) as:

> Even if schools can improve students' conduct while they are in school – and the evidence shows that they can indeed do that – the likelihood of lasting impact on the character of a child is diminished if the school's values aren't supported at home. For that reason, schools and families must come together in common cause. Working together, these two formative social institutions have real power to raise up moral human beings and to elevate the moral life of the nation.

The need for calm reason and policy is equally evident in a field necessarily linked with children's development, especially that of formal educational structures in society. Ultimately, the problems of school education are the problems of the family when it comes to inculcating particular values and virtues; the school cannot hope to substitute itself for the family, but it sometimes has to compensate for the failure of family life, and increasingly so. This is one reason why schools must clarify their aims: to put limits on their task.

3 Communitarianism and Education

In educational terms, communitarians are generally conservative, even though politically many are utopian and some are even populists.
(Robert Nash 1997:64)

In the education context of both America and Britain there is an emerging field of educational literature that draws on communitarianism. While communitarian thinkers define education broadly, in that education occurs in a range of institutions in addition to schools, the limited, but growing field of critical study has largely focused on the implications of communitarianism for education in schools. This is not surprising considering that all versions of communitarianism have important communal norms which are significant for educational theory, policy and practice. Within the liberal/communitarian debate this limited discussion of education to date centres on the contrast between schooling for the fulfilment of individual life plans against schooling to meet the collective needs of the community. Communitarians have argued that Western notions of education encourage individuals to compete against each other for material and symbolic advantages, and therefore schooling promotes individualism and generally ignores the moral claims that communities have on their members. This individualistic view of education, which promotes independence over loyalty, is also potentially subversive to the relationship between a child and the child's initial community: the family. There are often few ways in which children are encouraged to limit their individual choices for the good of the community or develop choices that serve the communal need. Some communitarians would also say that the State and market have failed to cultivate essential virtues and have undermined the moral underpinning once provided by the family and local community. They believe that the school can help by attempting to solve these tensions between individualism and community by promoting an education in, of, and by the local community for participation in democracy. However, there is a problem with this idea since as Walter Feinberg (1995) says: 'There are too many communities with too many different conceptions of the good, some of which are conflicting or mutually exclusive, to enable a pluralistic society to adopt a communitarian perspective as its only educational foundation'. He rejects the idea of a communitarian education, preferring instead to combine elements of communitarian understanding with the liberal view of education.

John Haldane (1995) regrets the fact that education in Britain has suffered as a result of not trying to understand communitarianism, and argues that the British philosophy of education will not improve unless it engages with the challenges of recent debates in moral philosophy. Haldane advocates a moderate form of communitarianism which is both 'pre-social nature' and 'intra-social self determination'. He believes that a person is both an individual and a social being and that education 'is a matter of conserving bodies of knowledge, sentiment and conduct, as these are incarnate in traditional practices' and that education is a 'social practice concerned with the transmission of certain traditional values'. His language is unmistakably of the communitarian theorist. He says (1995:83ff):

> Since learning ... is the correlative of being taught, what one learns is to a greater or lesser degree ways of seeing, understanding, valuing, imagining and behaving that are antecendently possessed by the teacher who is thereby authoritatively qualified with respect to them.

He makes clear that he does not aim to produce a system of social cloning or dent the critical capacity of children to think. Paul Theobald and Dale Snauwaert (1995:2) provide us with a short summary of the difference between the liberal and communitarian purpose of education:

> The fundamental purpose of communitarian education is the transmission of the cultural heritage, and with it enculturation into an ethic of association wherein there are fundamental obligations to the common good. In contrast, the fundamental purpose of liberal education is preparation for defining and pursuing one's own conception of the good life and with it enculturation into an ethic of tolerance wherein there is respect for the equal rights of others.

John Gray (1996) offers us a British communitarian liberal perspective of education in his work for the independent, left of centre, think-tank, DEMOS. It was DEMOS that sponsored a London lecture by Etzioni in 1995 and therefore introduced the political movement of communitarianism to Britain. Gray adopts the position that communitarianism enriches liberal philosophy with new and distinctive insights which owe few debts to the past. He rules out any return to 'traditional values' or to the 'traditional family' as pure nostalgia. Nevertheless, he makes a number of important points with which we can agree. For example, he believes that the ethos of schools is not that of the market exchange and that the marketization of education should be ended. He believes that real diversity within and between cultures, which would include the existence of faith-based schools, should be promoted actively. He believes that the State should have a clear commitment to the family, in all its diversity today, and that the State should ensure that the obligations of parenthood, including the responsibility to educate, are understood and accepted. He believes that access to good quality education should not be contingent on income and that, as a vital aid to equal opportunity, the allocation of opportunity should be meritocratic. On this last point, Gray favours the reintroduction of selection in State schools and advocates this as a communitarian liberal. In order to diminish the opting-out of the rich from State education he proposes that State education should be more 'inclusive'. This implies meritocratic selection which he believes will further social mobility without sacrificing social cohesion. Gray recognizes that any meritocratic criteria must take account of both special educational needs and disability, and he also recognizes that we need to raise the skills base of the most disadvantaged in society. His aim is no less than the creation of a strong public culture, rich in options, but embodied in common institutions, such as schools. He calls for a political debate in Britain on these issues, especially regarding how we are to reconcile diversity with commonality. His views may well form much of the agenda of New Labour's search for new education policies.

The main focus of Etzioni's moral project is the family and the importance of addressing what he views as the 'parenting deficit'. Schools are seen by public philosophy communitarians as the 'second line of defence' after families, and within the American context, communitarianism has contributed to the debate in education through its followers calling for the restoration of civic virtues. Indeed, in its 1991 statement the American communitarian movement included the following point: 'We *hold* that schools *can* provide essential moral education – without indoctrinating young people' (Etzioni 1995a:8). It is interesting that public philosophy communitarians use the terms *moral education* and *virtue* since both have received a bad press in educational literature, often being associated with a set of rules imposed on others. Nevertheless, Etzioni in all three of his books on communitarianism develops an argument for explicit character development and even character formation in schools. First, Etzioni discusses the concept of human nature, unfortunately, in a rather simplistic fashion. He presents two views of human nature; the first considers human nature as essentially benign, the product of Enlightenment thinking emphasizing progress and reason, and as a result of which children will naturally wish to learn; the second position, which views human nature as irrational and sinful, requires assertive inculcation of values through schooling, since a child's natural inclination when left to itself will be to reject learning. Etzioni then adopts what he calls a third view, which he describes as a developmental view of human nature. This view holds that people are born basically anti-social, but require a character education within the family and school to become virtuous. His attempt appears to hold out for an inclusive and open theory of the nature of human beings. He calls for schools to step in when families and neighbourhoods fail. As Etzioni (1997:92) says: 'schools are left with the task of making up for under-education in the family and laying the psychic foundations for character and moral conduct'. He believes that the purpose of education is the reinforcement of values gained in the home and the introduction of values to those children whose parents neglected their character formation.

Character and Values Education

Etzioni believes that many pupils in our schools have under-developed characters and that they are without firm commitments to values. He is very critical of the major influence that Jean Piaget and Lawrence Kohlberg have had on moral education. Both academics have been associated with values clarification which Etzioni believes is only suitable for people who already have evolved moral commitments. The chief function of values clarification methods is to allow children to identify their own beliefs by asking them to make choices given imaginary situations. It is based on a liberal individualism which proposes that children should learn moral skills and procedures. There is no conception of the good in this moral reasoning, only sets of rules about procedures to allow children to pursue their own vision of the good.

Piaget and Kohlberg were only interested in moral reasoning, not in the *internalization* of values. This values *internalization* is central to Etzioni's (1997:99) position and he explains it thus:

> What is missing between character formation (the ability to commit and guide oneself) and the development of moral reasoning is the *internalization* of (i.e., making part of oneself) commitments to a set of substantive values, to be achieved through moral education.

He calls for moral reconstruction within education, which means the development of basic personality traits in pupils. He recognizes the dangers of authoritarianism and the reluctance of teachers to engage in this process. Nevertheless, he insists that children who learn poor values within families and schools will become poor students and deficient workers, and he also questions the logic of the individual as an autonomous moral agent with no requirement to be committed to the collective. There is nothing new in this thinking, but he receives support from some psychologists such as Willard Gayling and Bruce Jennings who questioned the meaning of autonomy when they said:

> the culture of autonomy has created a strange chimera as its ideal: a free-standing individual for whom privacy and autonomy are sacred virtues, independent of his community, with almost unbridled authority over his actions and with no responsibility for its consequences. It has created a society of rights without duties or obligations: of authority without responsibility.
>
> (Gayling and Jennings 1996, Haste 1996)

James Wilson (1993:8) also condemns the 'values clarification' movement which he says leads teachers to avoid all hints of 'good' and 'right' or 'acceptable' and he calls this approach 'pedagogical idiocy'. These conservative authors, like a number of communitarians, are focusing on what they perceive as the weakened sense of social obligation among individuals to the communities in which they live. They argue that morality is not about the personal product of individual choice.

Etzioni effectively believes that the State should teach virtue and he claims that proper values are not being taught in schools. He does not tell us what these proper values are, nor does he offer any rational principles for the source of these values. He advocates self-esteem programmes in schools, which already exist throughout American primary education, in order to develop the character of the young. Many communitarians believe that educational professionals should train children in democratic decision-making and they also approve of the self-esteem programmes that encourage teachers to become expert at making children feel good about themselves. An important purpose of these self-esteem programmes is to develop group opinion and there is an assumption that children will always do the right thing. The aim is no less than developing a sense of equality, democracy and social justice in the young by removing racism, sexism and homophobia. Bruce Frohnen (1996:175) argues that much of the communitarian thought on education meshes perfectly with the thoughts of John Dewey who advocated democratic education and emphasized the egalitarian character of community.

What 'educational' methods do communitarians propose for the removal of sexism and racism from our classrooms? Frohnen (1996:164) observes that certain communitarians recommend public seminars, news conferences, personal confrontation and especially professionally orchestrated consciousness-raising. Frohnen says that Etzioni:

> endorses a plethora of mandatory workshops, 'cultural awareness' programs in which students are exposed to the ideology of multiculturalism, mandatory sensitivity training sessions for all students, and arbitration seminars in which those accused of insensitive remarks are exposed to large numbers of students, faculty, and administrators telling them that their views are offensive, harmful, and un-American. Using such means Etzioni argues, educational authorities can teach individuals the proper values without 'coercing' them.

There is clearly an authoritarian tone to these methods that Etzioni has obviously missed and perhaps even an illiberal content which combined have the potential to produce closed-mindedness and intolerance. Group opinions presented in this fashion could result in individual rights being subordinated to the claims of group interest and justice simply becoming the will of the stronger party.

A communitarian aim is undoubtedly to address the perceived disintegration of moral consensus in society which is principally caused by moral relativism. Some communitarians believe that the State school is still heavily dominated by 'values neutrality' and they recommend that we should train the young to develop the habits of acting morally. All of which sounds both reasonable and positive, even uncontroversial, but it may cause real conflict when implemented in practice. The values that many communitarians wish to see taught are intimately linked to the socialization of children and Philip Selznick (1987) observes that the central value of a communitarian morality is not freedom, but 'belonging'. Social and civic participation is the key to understanding a communitarian morality and Sandel (1984) believes it 'seeks to cultivate civic virtue, and to orient citizens to a common good beyond the sum of individual interests'. This would be achieved through teaching the values contained in the American Constitution and the Declaration of Independence with the justification that public schools are about the public and therefore must teach children to live in society. If the child does not participate then they are, by this reasoning, not full citizens. This again is problematic and raises the question of how children are to be motivated in order to participate in this great democratic enterprise. Communitarians often argue that it is in the individual's own interests to participate, but this is an instrumental argument that relies on liberal individualism for its justification. We know that schools teach values through the experience of being a school community and also through the curriculum. James Leming (1994) warns us that both didactic methods and children reasoning about moral issues are unlikely to succeed in changing behaviour by themselves. He draws our attention to the environment or ethos of schools and the types of expectations schools have of their children. He, and many others, believe that it is the ethos of schools that has the greater influence over human conduct and the forging of consensus, not the endless statements of values produced by State education authorities in America and Britain. New Labour's Social Exclusion Unit appears to share this view for it says that simply educating about sex does not prevent teenage pregnancies. Each year in Britain there are 9,000 births to under 16-year-olds – the highest rate in the Western world. The Unit is seeking to recruit teenage girls who will be credible messengers to persuade younger girls to 'Say No'.

Much of the communitarian appeal is essentially directed at State/public schools where there has been a renewed emphasis on character education and notions of good citizenship. In England and Wales there does appear to be the basis of a communitarian approach within the education system. Indeed, there was a strong tradition of character education in State schools as the *Board of Education Handbook of Suggestions for Teachers* in 1937 made clear: 'The purpose of the Public Elementary School is to form and strengthen character and develop the intelligence of the children entrusted to it'. The Handbook emphasized that the corporate life of the school should avoid anything that undermines character formation and listed the development of habits of industry, self-control, self-sacrifice, duty, respect for others, good manners, fair play and loyalty as the type of virtues to be encouraged. The dominant language of the Handbook is of moral conduct. While the substance of this tradition in education has largely been lost, the language and procedures are still evident in today's schools. Schools are today legally bound

- to have a daily act of worship in common;
- to provide a religious education programme that reflects the dominant Christian culture within society;
- to provide social, moral, cultural and spiritual education throughout the curriculum;
- to provide a sex education programme approved by the governors who are drawn from the local community and parents and
- to provide pastoral support and guidance for all pupils.

All these requirements are inspected and publicly reported on by an agency of the State. There are a number of difficulties with these requirements, not least that some of them are ignored by the teaching profession. Indeed, many no longer wish to see the authority of the State used to maintain Christianity. John Haldane (1986), a moderate British communitarian, believes that since we still have a Christian culture, we should teach Christianity. Teachers have enormous demands placed upon them by society and many teachers believe that their role is almost wholly concerned with cognitive learning – certainly not the formation of character in pupils. And yet the debate over whether our schools should teach morality is essentially misguided. Education is not value-free and while children would not learn morality by learning maxims or clarifying values, they do have their moral sense enhanced by being regularly induced by friends, family and schools to behave in accord with the most obvious standards of right conduct. These standards would include honesty, fair dealing, reasonable self-control and a set of core values which would more than likely correspond to the statement of values that the National Forum for Values in Education and the Community has produced.

The Forum, established by the School Curriculum and Assessment Authority in 1996, was charged with discovering whether there were any values upon which there is common agreement within society. While begun under a Conservative government, the Forum has the full support of the Labour government with Tony Blair advocating a fourth R – responsibility – to be taught in all schools. The Forum identified a number of values on which members believed society would agree and after extensive consultation with schools, parents and community members there was indeed overwhelming agreement on these values. This was certainly a communitarian approach since the only authority claimed for these values is the authority of consensus. The values excluded religious beliefs and were therefore not exhaustive. There are four general value areas identified consisting of self, relationships, society and the environment. Each of these areas has a general statement followed by a list of objectives for value-orientated behaviour and thinking. For example, under relationships the statement of values calls on us to respect others, to show others they are valued, to earn loyalty, to work cooperatively, to trust, to respect property, to resolve disputes peacefully, and so on. The difficulty with all the statements is that people will have different interpretations and applications of these values. If these value statements form the guidelines for schools, then each school community will have to decide how to interpret them within their own context. The Forum is an exponent of plural values. It was not interested in promoting the Christian morality, even in its most diluted form, which is part of our historic culture, since many of its members were broadly indifferent or even hostile to some aspects of Christian tradition. In effect the values identified by the Forum represent the promotion of secular ethicism and the end is seen to be human happiness by means of a materialistic humanism. The danger is that this weak communitarian approach may simply reinforce the trend that is leading to a form of materialistic humanism in education.

Henry Tam, who heads the Centre for Citizenship Development in Cambridge, states that the British communitarian movement is concerned with teaching values and the development of citizenship. He believes that there has been a number of well-established streams of independent British communitarian thought going back to Robert Owen that placed the value of human freedom in the context of mutual obligation which underpins social existence. Consequently, schools are being encouraged by British communitarians to take the values debate seriously since values are part of everyday life and are experienced and taken for granted through action. They call upon schools to foster social identity and encourage children to be responsible and caring individuals within their own communities. Only by doing so, they claim, will children learn the values of community and become effective members of democratic communities. This will require an active input from parents and schools. The values that Tam lists are almost identical to many which have been produced by the National Forum. Tam (1996) says:

> The key task for education is to teach young people to respect worthy traditional values, while enabling them to develop their critical capacity so that they can through democratic deliberations with others identify and strip away the prejudices which undermine doctrines of the past.

He leaves the question of how these values are to be integrated into the practices within education to another day. Nevertheless, we can see that the values Tam has in mind are secular and plural and that they ignore the Christian tradition. This secular approach is also a feature of the British community education movement which, like many modern communitarians, defined the purpose of education broadly in the early 1980s as:

> to foster the growth of loving persons, who are aware both of their own individuality and of their membership one of another; who accept one another, and who, understanding their own interdependent nature, choose to use their experience creatively in co-operation with one another.
>
> (see Keeble 1981:44)

British communitarians have not gone as far as Etzioni in terms of recommending the internalization of values in schools.

Communitarians who recommend character education have not been without their critics. Robert Nash (1997) for instance, argues that character education is a 'deeply and seriously flawed' project which is inherently authoritarian, excessively nostalgic, pre-modern in its understanding of virtue, aligned with conservative politics and anti-intellectual in its curricular content. Nevertheless, he hopes that, through sharing of perspectives, interpretation, and vocabularies, a sense of understanding and a possible 'shared moral reality' might emerge. Considering the long list of Nash's presuppositions it is difficult to see how this shared moral reality is achievable. A number of communitarians have advocated that we should focus more on educating parents on the basis that character formation begins before a child reaches the first year of primary education. Norton Garfinkle (1998) surveys recent research findings which document the fact that the first three years of life are critical for a child's moral development.

He proposes a 'communitarian solution' in which the national community take seriously this early development stage since, he claims, many children are being morally harmed before they arrive in formal schooling. He recommends a series of social policies that are designed to help children form moral characters, as he says:

> Children need to be exposed to caring role models – along with mentors and peers – in order to learn how to treat others with respect, dignity and compassion. Responsibility, self-discipline, truthfulness, fairness, compassion, and responsiveness to the needs of others: these are crucial ingredients of moral conduct. It is vital that they should be encouraged during the early childhood years – so that they can be reinforced then and later by the institutions of civil society, including schools and neighbourhood organisations.

Consequently, he recommends programmes of parental engagement and support, but where the family are 'expressing dysfunction' and 'children are suffering from inconsistent or damaging types of attachment', he proposes that society can provide 'sensitive remediation for the children'. No details of this 'sensitive remediation' are given beyond general statements about supporting the family. In extreme cases he suggests that the State should act *in loco parentis* to protect children from parental abuse. He recommends that character building should be planned and executed on a national basis, and he would not be averse to including some kind of national community service.

Michael Golby (1997) argues that the real aim of many communitarians is to connect young people more firmly with the world of employment and that moral behaviour for them is principally a matter of conforming to established norms. He is critical of communitarian approaches to education and even doubts whether schools have ever been formed and sustained by the local community. He forcefully argues that schools and teachers are not well placed to act decisively in the communitarian cause as 'second lines of defence' for, he argues, 'schools are more a result of the moral anarchy they are supposed by communitarians to combat than a solution to it'. He makes an exception for religious schools which he believes can be 'communities of place and memory'. However, in regard to State secular schools he is clear that they 'are ill-equipped in conditions of modernity to fulfil communitarian aims'.

Community Service

We have already seen how contradictions and problems are embedded within communitarian concepts of community. Etzioni's definition of community leaves us asking what constitutes the community? What are its boundaries? Whose interests does it promote? However, in terms of the school community it is precisely a community because its members are together actively sharing planned time and experiences. Like the family, it is not of our own choosing. Public philosophy communitarians place emphasis on the school as a community and view the school as providing a set of experiences to build moral character. Character is developed within a school community and therefore the messages they send to individuals, and the behaviour they encourage or discourage will influence the formation of character. As James Leming (1994) says:

> since the development of character involves the acceptance of norms valued by the community as binding on the individual, organisations [schools] characterised by *Gemeinschaft* are more ideally suited for the task of character education. Belonging to a *Gemeinschaft* community means essentially belonging to a moral community and living up to such norms as sharing, self-sacrifice, and collective responsibility. The individual in such social organisations values the quality of relationships and shares a concern with others for appropriate behaviour; one attempts to become a valued member of the normative community to maintain those significant relationships.

Relationships among members are valued in *Gemeinschaft* as ends in themselves, and the actions of individuals proceed from the express underlying communal identification. This process would involve parents and give priority to extra-curricular activities in which pupils could share experiences. The aim of the ethos of the school would be to build up a moral tenor and a sense of responsibility among the community members that would help children to act civilly and morally. There is clearly a strong concern for values and morality in much communitarian thought and an emphasis on education for citizenship and a desire to identify the shared core values that can be taught. However, how can this be achieved when many feel that the idea of the school as a community has declined?

In the early 1980s David Hargreaves (1982:34–5) wrote *The Challenge for the Comprehensive School* in which he described how a teacher from an inner-city school observed:

> The school's not like it was. We used to be like a family, the old style working-class community. We didn't have to do anything special: we just drew on what was there in the home background. But it's not like that any more. And there's not much we can do about it. How can you make a community in a school when there's no community out there?

Hargreaves detailed how schools had lost their corporate vocabulary because phrases such as 'team spirit', '*espirit de corps*' and 'loyalty to the school' had declined in favour of a culture of individualism. He berated the modern comprehensive school for not making more of a contribution to the social solidarity of society. In many respects his book presented a communitarian agenda in education and we shall return to some of his ideas for the curriculum. In the meantime, many American communitarians have suggested that a year of community service would foster and reinforce shared experiences and would be an antidote to the ego-centred mentality of youth.

Communitarians in the USA have campaigned openly to make 'national service' mandatory for all school children. They believe that volunteer programmes, while extremely useful, attract a small minority and are therefore inadequate in meeting the requirements of society. President Bush established a Commission on National and Community Service in 1990 which published a report, *What You Can Do For Your Country*, strongly endorsing community service programmes (see Rosario and Franklin 1994). Most communitarian ideas of community or national service are viewed within the context of civic education or citizenship and their aim is intimately linked with children learning the meaning of social interdependence and democratic principles. They believe that civic education must include experiential learning of the kind offered by community service and Etzioni (1995b:113) calls it the 'capstone of a student's educational experience' in school. Benjamin Barber (1991) outlines the aims of this 'national service' by indicating that it is 'an indispensable prerequisite of citizenship and thus a condition for democracy's preservation'. He strongly advocates mandatory programmes and insists that no one should be exempt from them. He provides a long list of benefits of such national service which include: serving the public interest or good; teaching about rights and responsibilities; teaching liberty; eliminating ignorance, intolerance, and prejudice; and empowering students to participate in society. He believes such programmes should be communal as well as community-based, in the sense that the students learn to form a community of service amongst themselves by working in teams. The programme would be organized around an academic course taught in the classroom and there would be a number of options from which students would be free to choose. He also suggests that there should be incentives to help students continue this type of public service after the mandatory period has ended. There are few such programmes in America and in England it is more likely that students experience a compulsory 'business experience' in a work placement than any sustained and integrated period of community service as part of their school curriculum. There are of course many critics of this particular communitarian idea of 'national service'.

In Britain a few politicians have called for national service schemes. Leo McKinstry (1997:146), a former prominent Islington Labour councillor, has advocated the establishment of a nation-wide scheme of compulsory community service, which would, he says, encourage young people to think about their wider social responsibilities. Like some communitarians in the USA, he believes that a scheme of national service should be mandatory for all, since he says that voluntary schemes are only suitable for well-motivated young people; disaffected youth in inner cities are the least likely to participate in voluntary programmes. Significantly, he also advocates that the British Army should play its full part in this project through the establishment of more cadet organizations and the expansion of the Territorial Army, and concludes that there could be 'special recruitment drives by the Territorial Army in the inner cities to attract those who would benefit most from a disciplined environment'. It seems that McKinstry has, like many communitarians, given up on families and schools, and advocates State provision of compulsory programmes of service which teach discipline and conformity, especially for the poor and disaffected in our inner cities. It no doubt also has the implicit aim of removing the unemployed from the streets and perhaps even reducing crime. The intention of such national service would be the formation of a civic consciousness, but communitarians need to be aware of the social control function exercised in the name of the community. McKinstry's views are deeply paternalistic. British youth are familiar with a number of government employment training programmes that have not been entirely optional or successful. Compulsory national service would simply be an extension of these low-skilled training programmes and would be of more benefit to big business. Maryland is the only State in the USA to have made community service a requirement of high school graduation and it is interesting how the communitarian, David Anderson (1998:42), makes the link between community service and the world of work. He says: 'In the Communitarian school a new spirit of community would exist, one which would connect children to their teachers and their parents and, significantly to their parents' employers'. Anderson emphasizes the collective responsibility theme that animates communitarian thinking and suggests that bridges between government, the market and civil society should be strengthened.

Indeed, the influence of big business can be detected in the language that has been imposed on schools. We used to describe the school as a community; today many believe it to be little more than an enterprise. We can see how our modern education system views knowledge as a commodity to be bought and sold, as opposed to knowledge viewed as service, not to be acquired for power or wealth. Knowledge seen as property to be selected and promoted according to its exchange value in the market is gaining an ascendancy, while knowledge used as a means of self-fulfilment which develops a cultural and social responsibility appears to be in decline. Head teachers are praised for their entrepreneurial skills in hiring out school property or running the school as a small business, while less attention is focused on the head teacher as a leader of an educational community with the school used as a free resource to the local community. Students are increasingly viewed as 'units of resource' or clients/customers rather than as unique individuals endowed with reason and conscience. Schools are also encouraged to view other schools as competitors, or even as the enemy. Competition between schools is the order of the day. Schools are not encouraged to emphasize collectivity, collegiality, cooperation and sharing. Parents are encouraged to think that they have choice when in actual fact it is increasingly the case that it is the schools which choose the pupils. Parental choice of school is meaningless if it is not a free, conscious and deliberate selection. Education is also being privatized with 'voluntary' contributions being extracted from parents which blurs what the State should provide and undermines education as a basic human right. How can communitarian ideas seriously influence an education system so dominated by these market forces?

The School Curriculum

The educational goals described by Hargreaves (1982) for comprehensive schools sought to increase greater democratic participation, stimulate greater social solidarity and help resolve conflict between different communities. All three goals sit extremely well with communitarian thinking on education. He believed that if education was to contribute to a sense of greater social solidarity then we had to revisit the questions of what sort of society we wanted and how can education help us realize such a society? Education, for him, had become overly concerned with the cult of the individual and the content of education had increasingly moved in a technical and depersonalized direction. Hargreaves did not think that the culture of individualism in education had been an error *in toto*, only that it had become too dominant and had ignored the social functions of education which he summarizes: 'if an excessive and exclusive attention to social and societal needs jeopardises the education of the individual, then an excessive and exclusive attention to individual needs jeopardises those of society'. The consequence of the modern obsession with individuals is that teachers assume, wrongly, that the good society will be created through the education of good individuals. One possible solution he suggested was a community-centred curriculum of which community studies, including practical community service, were an integral part. He did not want this community-centred curriculum to become a mere appendage to the traditional curriculum, nor limited to the less able in schools. Therefore, he proposed that it should be compulsory for all and that it should consist of a core of traditional subjects organized around community studies. He believed that external examinations had far too much influence over the secondary curriculum and that this influence should be reduced in favour of increased internal assessment in schools. He believed that traditional school subjects should be more integrated with each other and that teachers should consequently develop team teaching strategies. The curriculum, in Hargreaves model, would consist of a series of general objectives that would translate into a flexible timetable and core subjects would be reshaped into new forms and contexts.

All of this was a radical rethinking of the traditional school curriculum in an attempt to help all children, of whatever ability, to be active members of their communities for, as Hargreaves says (1982:144), the purpose of the school curriculum is to provide children with the knowledge and skills required for them to participate effectively in all of these different kinds of communities because 'it is when we belong to many groups and communities, and play an active role within them, that we are most likely to learn about them, and resolve, the tension between solidarity and conflict'. The function of schools is to prepare children for membership of several communities and in anticipation of this, the school needs to offer opportunities within it for children to experience different kinds of community groupings and learn about how to resolve conflict between them. Hargreaves admits that this is a bold vision and a daunting challenge, but believes nevertheless that schools need to increase community participation; he asks: 'what other major agency apart from the school has any hope of success?' His book also promoted the idea of the themes of citizenship and moral education in schools. Hargreaves's proposed curriculum is in many ways a working out of a communitarian agenda for the school curriculum and education, although he would not have called it that in 1982.

Tom Bentley (1998), writing in a DEMOS-sponsored publication, has produced a widely publicized text on education which develops many of Hargreaves's ideas for the late 1990s with a more distinctly communitarian approach, although his text does not once refer to communitarianism. Bentley speaks of 'active, community-based learning' (p. 30) which is aimed at developing a capacity in individuals to be responsible independent learners. He details a range of volunteering opportunities for young people, many of which are geared towards preparation for employability. He also says that young people should be given real responsibility through devolving a range of decision-making to them so that positive learning can take place in genuine communities. Schools, he says, should appoint 'school-community co-ordinators' (p. 72) and that they should eventually evolve into 'neighbourhood learning centres' (p. 186) which welcome every learner and 'combine the social, cultural, financial, informational and human resources of their local communities with those of a publicly funded, professionally staffed education system'. His text also places emphasis on the educational and social demands of a modern economy for 'employability' and therefore he is concerned about providing workers with the necessary skills to place Britain in a position of international economic competitiveness. Bentley's ideas, which also make no reference to communitarian thinkers, are certainly challenging, but they lack detail and by continually emphasizing 'new ways' without explaining how these ideas would work in practice renders them rather like other communitarian-based ideas – composed largely of policy rhetoric. New Labour has already begun to develop some of these ideas, for example, by suggesting the establishment of 'neighbourhood learning centres' in its Green Paper on *Supporting Families* (1998). Consequently, Bentley's other reflections will no doubt further expand the debate about the future of education policy.

The 1990s have seen a more centralized and traditional curriculum in secondary schools which is contrary to the proposals advocated by Hargreaves. If most British communitarians believe that communities must be preserved and that it is important to teach traditional values then would they also agree, for example, that the National Curriculum in history should continue to consist mainly of British history? The majority of what is taught as history in schools is largely foreign to the private memories and personal experiences of children, but what is taught supplements their memories and experiences with public and political histories that provide a common memory. What then do communitarians have to say to us about 'Britishness' as a value in education or as a part of our settled traditions and personal identity? Very little it seems. In America some communitarians would object to an approach to history teaching which is particularistic – that is, which encourages children to seek their identity in the cultures of their ancestors. Other communitarians emphasize that all children within a particular country should be at least introduced to the 'national culture' to which they should 'belong'.

Diane Ravitch (1991) describes a California history syllabus with a section on 'National Identity' which advocates that history should be taught in such a way as to help American children realize that patriotism celebrates the moral force of the American idea of the nation that unites as one people the descendants of many cultures, races, religions, and ethnic groups. Communitarians often use school-based history as a tool for teaching their 'modern virtues' which is intended to help children reject their racist and sexist pasts in favour of some sort of cultural egalitarianism. Michael Johnson (1995) offers a rationale for this by advocating a form of communitarian education which seeks to promote a love of learning and a tradition of excellence and believes that:

> this love of learning and one's culture's traditions of excellence must finally be based in a love of the local place, the local community, the local people, no matter how small the place or humble the community and its people. Otherwise, our young will continue to learn their modern lessons of disdain for their folkways, their homeplaces, and the common people in our nation's schools. And we will 'educate' still another generation of 'rootless,

emancipated, migrating individuals', who are 'cultural renegades believing in nothing but their own right to a good time'.

However, with so much social fragmentation in Britain, it is often the school curriculum that bears the main burden of transmitting the national idea for many children and of course not all school subjects contribute equally to fostering a national identity. History has often been singled out as the subject that helps young people understand the shared values which are a distinctive feature of British society, but communitarians in Britain are silent on what should be taught.

The National Curriculum

In the process of revising the National Curriculum in England and Wales the government has recognized the need for a more explicit rationale for the school curriculum and the place of the National Curriculum within it. The government has sought to include more explicit provision in the areas of citizenship education, personal, social and health education, and the spiritual, moral, social and cultural dimensions of the curriculum. A series of aims and purposes of the school curriculum have been devised to form the preamble to the National Curriculum itself and these aims appear to fit well with a communitarian view of education. The school curriculum is now expected to promote a belief in the democratic principles of fairness and equality; an understanding of the rights and duties and responsibilities of living in a democratic society; the need to combat social exclusion by raising educational expectations and to promote social cohesion, community involvement and a sense of social responsibility. The school curriculum is expected to provide pupils with opportunities to develop a sense of identity, respect, tolerance and empathy through knowledge and appreciation of their own social and cultural heritage and traditions, and of the culture and traditions of people in other communities, countries, societies, ethnic groups, faiths and beliefs. In a direct reference to the work of the National Forum on Values, there are recommendations in the National Curriculum that opportunities be made available in schools to develop pupils spiritually and morally and formulate values relating to *self, relationships and society*. While many of these educational goals remain quite general or even fuzzy, they appear to enjoy widespread support.

The New Labour government has stamped its ethical mark on schools by incorporating a series of ambiguous words and phrases into the written aims, purposes and values underpinning the National Curriculum. This is surely a consequence of the influence communitarianism has had on the hierarchy of the Party, but it is a version of communitarianism which is both conservative and morally prescriptive. New Labour expects schools and teachers to train the citizens of the future; inculcate into pupils appropriate social and moral values and dispositions; promote, as a 'good thing', duty and responsibilities to the community; advance the common good and foster the creation and stability of common values to deal with fragmentation. Inclusion and social cohesion is principally seen by New Labour as a question of shared morals, not material circumstances. Consequently, redistribution of wealth and social equality receive low priority in New Labour's version of communitarianism. Schools are to remain in competition with each other for *the right* applicants; will continue to be subject to rigorous inspection, tests, and published league tables; progressive teaching methods will continue to be disparaged; and the government will remain even more obsessed with its crusade to raise standards. Parents are also to be blamed for their children's non-attendance at school; for their non-completion of homework; and even for allowing their children out on the street beyond a time which could be set by the local council. Private companies will be encouraged to run failing schools for profit and schools will remain highly differentiated in governance. New Labour has certainly shifted in a distinctly 'New Market' direction on education policy, which is why Stephen Driver and Luke Martell (1997) conclude that: 'If communitarianism is New Labour's answer to Thatcherism, so too is it Tony Blair's rebuff to Old Labour'. In summary, New Labour recognizes moral diversity, but appears to desire the unity of moral consensus and is prepared to place a great deal of the responsibility for achieving this on the school curriculum.

However, the messages from New Labour are also confusing and contradictory. Nicholas Tate, the government's Chief Executive of the Qualifications and Curriculum Authority, has recently adopted a very clear communitarian tone in his pronouncements. In a speech delivered at King's College, London in November 1998 he claims that we lack, both as individuals and as a society, a shared account of who we are, where we come from and where we are going (Tate 1998). As a result, we fall back on narrow utilitarian explanations of the purpose of education which, he says, are insufficient. He sets out seven 'big ideas' for education which are intended to balance the government's other 'big ideas' on standards, literacy and numeracy. They are as follows:

First, education is about aspiring to high ideals of human behaviour. It is not morally neutral about what it is to be a human person. Second, liberal states see education as helping to move us towards the kind of society in which we wish to live. This involves reasserting the place of community in our collective lives. It also involves confidence in shared values. Third, the ends of education are not purely utilitarian. It is not just about 'getting on'. Fourth, is it about employability, in the broadest sense of the word. Fifth, it is not just about things that are quantifiable and measurable. Sixth, it is about valuing knowledge. Seventh, it is about helping us to develop a sense of plural identities in an increasingly confusing world.

(Tate 1998: para. 56)

This could have been written or said by almost any American communitarian. It is an attempt to be much more explicit about the values in the school curriculum, but there is a huge gulf between this type of rhetoric and the reality of an English education system still dominated by utilitarian approaches. The contradictions and confusions are set to continue for some time to come.

Conclusion

Many communitarians see morality from the perspective of the community and rights are both derivative and secondary. For them the morality of liberalism is too abstract and rational. Feinberg (1995) describes how a liberal morality 'is not grounded in either practice or tradition, but pretends to be rooted in the rational faculty of the individual, a faculty which somehow cuts across tradition and is supposed to refine, check, and alter tradition'. A number of communitarians would argue that this is an incorrect conception of reason, but then suggest that our moral language should serve the national community, perhaps as a national morality. Which is more dangerous? Selznick (1987) believes that communitarians owe a debt to the achievements of liberalism and that communitarians should assimilate these achievements within their new framework, but he thinks that a communitarian idea of morality is still in its infancy. In the end what we are left with are more questions than answers. How can communitarianism's perspective on morality, based as it is on communal norms, change society through the efforts of schools?

Hargreaves's approach seeks to increase the solidarities in the various communities that comprise democratic society and educate them to resolve their conflicts through a school curriculum based on community-centred studies. He is critical of the progressive individualism that has led to the ethical individualism in schools and proposes that genuine individuality must be rooted in group life and result from direct experience of community life. This would entail that schools should be smaller in size and engage their students with a focus on investigating their local community. The assumptions behind these recommendations by Hargreaves are that children will feel fulfilled by discussing issues in groups, that they will be more empowered and will increase their self-esteem, which together will bring out their innate sociability thereby creating a more egalitarian society. He also argues, as do many communitarians, that the experiences in schooling are more effective than teaching. Robert Nash (1997:72–3) provides an interesting, but useful, summary of what he believes to be the essential features of a communitarian curriculum for schools:

> Generally, the communitarian curriculum is a culturally conservative one, with the possible exception of its emphasis on public service. It includes most of the traditional subjects embodied in the liberal arts ... the communitarian curriculum organises these subjects in such a way as to encourage students' loyalty to the values of their local and national communities. To this end, the communitarian curriculum is rich in literature, history, and religion – content that is a particularly strong reinforcer of the sense of community, tradition, transcendence, and civic responsibility that all young people will need to develop in order to become excellent human beings and good democratic citizens. The communitarian curriculum also includes subject matter that is critical of the principle of liberal individualism whenever it intentionally or unintentionally threatens to trump the value of communal identity.

Certainly, there is a strong tendency for re-education programmes in much communitarian thought. For many communitarians, education must first be in character. The new National Curriculum, to be implemented in 2000, appears to contain some aims from a communitarian perspective on education, but has little concrete to say about learning experiences beyond the classroom. The school curriculum will still focus on a limited core of academic subjects that do not reflect the full spread of human potential and ability. It is precisely why Bentley (1998:1) argues forcefully that education in school must become broader by including 'a wider range of learning experience, experience of roles and situations which mirror those we value in society', so that 'students can apply what they learn in situations beyond the bounds of their formal educational experience'. Tony Blair in his 1998 political manifesto, *The Third Way: New Politics for the New Century* (p. 12), also emphasizes State control of education:

> Strong communities depend on shared values and a recognition of the rights and duties of citizenship – not just the duty to pay taxes and obey the law, but the obligation to bring up children as competent, responsible citizens, and to support those – such as teachers – who are employed by the state in the task. In the past we have tended to take such duties for granted. But where they are neglected, we should not hesitate to encourage and even enforce them, as we are seeking to do with initiatives such as our home–school contracts between schools and parents.

Blair goes on to talk about appropriate levels of State intervention and about the State's powers of intervention. The idea that teachers are State employees who are responsible for educating future citizens gives further emphasis to State control of education. We therefore need to look further at education in school, in particular at citizenship education and the common good in relation to schooling and the communitarian agenda.

4 Citizenship Education and the Common Good

> How are we to bring children to the spirit of citizenship and humanity which is postulated by democratic societies? By the actual practice of democracy at school. It is unbelievable that at a time when democratic ideas enter every phase of life, they should have been so little utilized as instruments of education.
>
> (Jean Piaget, *The Moral Judgement of the Child* 1965)

Citizenship education and the common good in schools are two key concepts in the communitarian agenda in education. While the previous chapter discussed character education and community service within the school curriculum, communitarian thinking extends further than these, encompassing both preparation for citizenship and the promotion of the common good. From the communitarian perspective citizenship and the common good have an integrative function in society. Citizenship is concerned with the social relationships between people and the relationships between people and the institutional arrangements afforded by the State and society. Therefore, according to many communitarians, citizens need a society with a degree of common goals and a sense of the collective common good. Within this thinking, the citizen earns the right of citizenship through his or her participation in society and attending to the duties and responsibilities that become the defining characteristics of the practices of citizenship in this view. The difficulty with this notion of citizenship is that it is a status that needs to be earned, and therefore can be lost. Anthony Giddens (1998:65) describes it in another way as 'no rights without responsibilities' and says that this is the motto of the new politics of the Third Way. While many communitarians strongly argue that the State should create opportunities to empower citizens and that the local community should encourage participation through example, nevertheless, the problem of how to motivate people to become active citizens with a concern for the collective good is daunting, especially for teachers.

Within education there is also the problem that certain people may continue to be excluded and this may further impede their full incorporation into the political community. This raises the question of what activities do we define as the measure of active or good citizenship in schools? If citizenship is differentiated, it no longer provides a shared experience or common status. Apportioning the responsibilities for the task of schooling is clearly a task shared between parents, professionals and the State acting on behalf of the citizen pupil. Communitarians invariably stress the role of the community and Adrian Oldfield (1990:173) says:

> The idea of community has less to do with formal organisation than with a sense of belonging and commitment. The commitment is to others who share interests, or positions, or purposes, and it is also to those who, for whatever reason, are unable to look after their own interests or pursue their own purposes. It is to seek the good of others at the same time as, and sometimes in neglect of, one's own good. It is to approach social relationships in an Aristotelian spirit of 'concord'. It is this that creates the sense of community; and it is this that creates citizens.

In other words, the sense of the common good will help prevent the deliberate exclusion of individuals from the community, but there remains the problem of generating sufficient commitment among enough individuals to establish the common good within a community, however the 'common good' is defined.

Citizenship Education

Citizenship education has always held a place, albeit a haphazard one, in British education, but not as a discrete subject in the school curriculum. Currently it is provided in schools as one of the five cross-curricular themes and schools are obliged to have a written policy on education for citizenship, but practice varies considerably. Ken Fogelman's (1998:47) survey of schools confirmed that many are doing something and that few said they are doing nothing on citizenship education. Nevertheless, Osler and Starkey (1996:76) believe that 'too much that goes under the heading of education for citizenship is low status, poorly organised, unpopular with students and teachers and ineffective'. There has indeed been much criticism of the ways in which young people have been prepared by schools for their citizenship role. Successive governments have expressed repeated concern at the apathy among young people, especially their growing tendency not to exercise their right to vote in democratic elections. This often narrowly equates the notion of citizenship with the idea of the *elector*. It is interesting to note that when education for citizenship has been raised in the past it has usually been associated with a perceived crisis in society (Stradling 1987). Many politicians are also concerned about our British identity within the modern nation state, which they perceive to have been weakened, and they also wish to promote the legitimacy of the present democratic system of government in Britain through the active involvement of all its citizens. Indeed, the New Labour government is embarking on an ambitious programme of constitutional reforms that call for even greater participation, initially through referenda for devolved bodies, but extending to quasi-non-governmental organizations. The State is anticipating greater citizenship participation in the future against a background of general distrust in the institutions, politicians and bureaucrats who govern society.

However, there is no comprehensive list of citizen rights in Britain and no list of corresponding duties; in a sense, there are no citizens, only subjects of the crown, which leaves legal definitions of citizenship vague. The appearance of Citizens' Charters in recent years merely extends the notion of citizenship to mean customer or user of services. Moreover, for those people who experience major impediments to their participation as full citizens through long-term unemployment and social disadvantage, talk of citizenship can be meaningless, especially when there is little priority to discuss the resources needed to enable individuals to become effective citizens. What are the minimum conditions that the State should provide for effective citizenship with reference to education, housing, income, health, employment, freedom of speech and association, etc.? Some politicians even appear to think that citizenship education offers a panacea to solve society's problems and approach the concept itself in a simplistic way, failing to recognize that it is both complex and contested – as the many critics of T.H. Marshall's classic study of citizenship in 1950 demonstrate (see Heater 1990, Dynneson and Gross 1991, McLaughlin 1992, Sears 1996, Rauner 1997). There have also been a number of pressure groups, such as the Citizenship Foundation and the Council for Education in World Citizenship, which have strongly campaigned for the increased prominence of citizenship education in schools.

Within this context the Labour government established an advisory group under the chairmanship of Professor Bernard Crick – a staunch campaigner for citizenship education in schools – to produce a statement of the aims of citizenship education in schools as well as a broad framework of what good citizenship education might look like from the infant school onwards. The Labour government accepted the recommendations of the final Advisory Group on Education for Citizenship and the Teaching of Democracy, and is set to introduce citizenship education and the teaching of democracy as a formal part of the National Curriculum in State schools. The advisory group (QCA 1998) recommended citizenship education as a statutory entitlement for 5–16-year-olds from the year 2000, with schools required to demonstrate how they are fulfilling this obligation through tightly defined learning outcomes which are to be inspected objectively. The advisory group did not recommend a particular curriculum for citizenship education, but focused instead on an output model of the curriculum (learning outcomes) that allows for different approaches involving different subject combinations based on existing good practice in schools. The advisory group accepted the general move towards making all aspects of the curriculum, including citizenship education, both more explicit and measurable through the inspection of learning outcomes. These outcomes will include knowledge of: democratic practices and institutions; parties; pressure groups and voluntary bodies; world affairs and global issues; taxation and expenditure.

Citizenship education is, therefore, to include the knowledge, skills and values relevant to the nature and practices of participative democracy. In effect, citizenship education will be used as a device to cultivate a sense of community and purpose among the young. Crick's advisory group stressed that programmes of citizenship education should focus on community involvement and that it should take place in and out of school. The advisory group meant three things by 'effective education for citizenship':

> Firstly, children learning from the very beginning self-confidence and socially and morally responsible behaviour both in and beyond the classroom, both towards those in authority and towards each other ... Secondly, learning about and becoming helpfully involved in the life and concerns of their communities, including learning through community involvement and service to community ...

Thirdly, pupils learning about and how to make themselves effective in public life through knowledge, skills and values.

(QCA 1998:11–13)

By defining the aims of citizenship education as social and moral responsibility, community involvement and political literacy and by recommending that it be a statutory entitlement for all pupils in State schools, the advisory group has offered its own conception of the good life. Part of this conception is that liberal democratic skills and virtues must be taught. Schools will be judged on this and whether the programmes of citizenship education in each school actually modifies the behaviour of the pupils in an 'appropriate' direction. Already OFSTED (Office for Standards in Education) inspectors comment on and judge the ethos of schools, which includes how the children interact socially and morally with each other in and out of the classroom. The advisory group outlined that

a main aim for the whole community should be to find or restore a sense of common citizenship, including a national identity that is secure enough to find a place for the plurality of nations, cultures, ethnic identities and religions long found in the United Kingdom. Citizenship education creates common ground between different ethnic and religious identities.

The advisory group has adopted the understanding that a refusal to prescribe the content of citizenship education would in itself reduce the potential for conflict and disagreement amongst teachers and parents. However, there are a number of issues surrounding the recommendations of the advisory group that are both complex and unresolved.

One of the key issues is how citizenship is to be balanced with broader personal, social and moral education. In addition to establishing an advisory group on education for citizenship, the Secretary of State for Education also created four other national advisory committees as part of the review of the National Curriculum in schools. These included groups on: sustainable development education; creative and cultural education; personal, social and health education; and QCA's own revision of spiritual, moral, social and cultural development, which is already a statutory requirement of the curriculum. There is obviously great scope for overlap and duplication in the work of these advisory groups and it is not entirely clear whether these groups were well co-ordinated and integrated. They certainly deliberated separately and produced their own reports and recommendations. QCA then established a Preparation for Adult Life Group to develop an overview of the recommendations of each national advisory group. These national groups were concerned with 'life-skills' subject areas and all of them are to have a more explicit role in the National Curriculum. The personal, social and health education group has recommended that a non-statutory Code of Practice containing learning objectives and learning experiences for all key stages should be published as guidance for schools, while the group on sustainable development has recommended the publication of learning outcomes for each key stage to raise awareness of this area. The group on creative and cultural education has recommended that these dimensions of the curriculum should be strengthened through a more explicit statement of the key purposes and principles for the school curriculum. QCA's initiative on spiritual, moral, social and cultural development is already being piloted in schools.

However, citizenship education appeared to have priority and was the only group that recommended statutory learning outcomes; the government insisted that citizenship education is complementary to and not a substitute for personal, social and moral education. The definition of citizenship education adopted by the advisory group can best be summarized in Derek Heater's (1990:336) words that 'a citizen is a person furnished with knowledge of public affairs, instilled with attitudes of civic virtue, and equipped with skills to participate in the political arena'. What intellectual coherence will this new citizenship education have? Since the advisory group aimed at 'no less than a change in the political culture of this country both nationally and locally', how can it avoid accusations of indoctrination? Citizenship education is intimately connected with the essential nature of morality, community and identity and will therefore be a contested life-skills subject area. What type of education is citizenship education and how can it lead to the formation of knowledgeable citizens aware of the ethical and political principles on which our democracy is founded and who will freely involve themselves in national and local civic life?

The Contested Aims of Citizenship Education

Bellah (1991) believes that citizenship education should not involve self-interest but is instead created by the search for 'social justice'. Some British teachers share this view and the danger remains that they may select and deliver a citizenship education programme of abstractly defined principles of justice and rights that is little more than political propaganda. Parents may also object to certain sensitive aspects of the content of citizenship education programmes and in the name of liberty attempt to block a school's fulfilment of its own understanding of its legal obligations. Schools cannot teach citizenship education without exposing children to different ways of life and this exposure may conflict with their religious or other beliefs. Therefore, do parents have the right to shield their children from being educated about different ways of life? The answer appears to be a limited yes. Section 17 of the Education Reform Act 1988 provides for some 'safeguards' for schools by allowing 'exception clauses' or 'specified modifications' to be made to the National Curriculum, which would include any programme of citizenship education. The Secretary of State for Education would arbitrate on any decisions regarding such exceptions. Some schools could be made exempt from some parts of the mandatory National Curriculum school requirement. However, this is unlikely as the only group to use this clause of the Act successfully was the Catholic Church and that was a limited 'exception' which allowed Catholic schools to teach about contraception within the context of Catholic teaching. There are also a number of other issues with regard to the respective roles of parents and the State *vis-à-vis* the education of children. While we may agree that schools have an obligation to develop some appreciation of the importance of key democratic values, citizenship education will remain a problematic area for teachers and parents. The advisory group merely offers guidance on the teaching of controversial issues.

A State mandated citizenship education programme is not neutral. The government claims that it is not attempting to impose on all schools a national curriculum of citizenship education. However, its learning outcomes presuppose non-neutral accounts of the human good. By publishing centrally determined and defined goals of what is to be learnt in citizenship education while still allowing the freedom for each school to decide how such learning is to occur, the government is really saying: 'You are free to do what we say in any way you choose'. The result will be a great diversity of courses especially in an education system that lacks a common school for all. In addition, inspectors will employ the 'output' model to judge whether the goals are being achieved, but the success of a good citizenship education programme may well depend more on the argument, the evidence and the debate rather than on the specified outcomes. Many teachers have already expressed concern that OFSTED often ignores the fact that in schools people and ideas, not quantifiable objects, are the 'output'. It is also easier to assess cognate learning than measure progress in affective learning, which means that teachers will inevitably focus their attention on the testable components.

Citizenship education, as defined by the advisory group, is concerned with social relationships between people and relationships between people and institutions. It emphasizes the development of human beings as social agents who are interdependent with one another. It is about social and personal education and, above all, the integration of the person into society. The State, through its specified learning outcomes, will seek to encourage some character traits in school children and not others. Consequently, the government views children in our society as future citizens and parents will therefore have a limited authority over their children and will certainly not be able to impede the State's promotion of civic loyalty. Citizenship education certainly implies a commitment to openness and accountability, and to developing the competence of political literacy and participation skills coupled with skills to effect change. However, it would also seem reasonable that parental convictions that conflict with teaching children certain aspects of civic virtues should be tolerated. To what extent, then, has the State the right to intrude into the familial, communal and religious ways of life for the sake of educating full-scale citizens of the future? Parents will not be allowed to invoke a 'conscience clause', like that available to them for religious education teaching, in order to withdraw their children from citizenship education classes. It seems that in a democracy parents cannot prevent children from being educated to exercise full rights of citizenship or choosing from among diverse life styles. The argument in support of this view is that children may be introduced to certain ideas but without necessarily accepting them. While children are more than the creatures of their parents, there needs to be some limit on the loyalty demanded by the State, especially when the State demands actions from its citizens which some may believe to be immoral. Further, citizenship is only one of a number of identities that the individual possesses.

Citizenship education focuses on the development of children as citizens in order to form citizens who participate in their local communities and understand their rights and exercise their duties to society. Citizenship education is more than the minimal conditions of reasonable public judgement. It includes mutual respect amongst citizens of different religions, race, genders, ethnicity. This is a key area of the communitarian agenda in education. The liberal view of citizenship education focuses on the status of the individual as a rights bearer and attempts to maintain guiding principles to regulate the lives of citizens. Citizens need, in this view, to acquire certain skills to participate in debate and protest within a democracy. The primary idea is to promote a commitment to autonomy and to agree a set of minimum rules established by the State. Citizens have the right to place their private commitments ahead of their right to participate in community or public life. This liberal view allows the individual to pursue individual interests within a set of shared procedural rules, but practical decisions cannot be derived from a set of rules. However, agreement on these procedural rules will involve some substantive view of what is right or just, something liberals claim they avoid. Liberals claim that they confine themselves to the aims for education which all citizens can be presumed to accept, but this leaves the education for the specific and distinctive conceptions of the good to individuals. Liberal conceptions of education also presuppose their own set of virtues. For many young people the idea that they have a responsibility to be involved in formal activities within their community can be justified on the basis of individualism, through the ulterior motive of self-development which is a commitment to the self rather than society.

The Commission on Citizenship, established by the Conservative government in 1990 adopted this liberal view and said: 'We consider that citizenship involves the perception and maintenance of an agreed framework of rules or guiding principles, rather than shared values' (1990:13). The liberal New Right also adopt this view since they are committed to individualism and the reduction of the influence of the State. This stance contrasts with conservative New Right proponents who would accept a closer relationship between the State and the individual citizen. Communitarian and liberal views agree that citizenship education refers to a democratic normative ideal which holds that the governed should be full and equal participants in the political process. However, communitarian views place greater emphasis on duties and the belief that citizens should sacrifice part of their private life for the benefit of the whole community. Altruism is encouraged, as is commitment to others, as a natural motive for involvement in community. In communitarian approaches citizens are still seen as individual members of a community with rights, but communitarians would add shared values, common interests and obligations. However, how far should the citizens' duties extend? There is potentially an unlimited number of responsibilities and obligations.

The view of citizenship education outlined by the government's advisory group could be seen as essentially a communitarian approach. It seeks to encourage teachers to help children practise citizenship in schools as part of their formal education. It also positions children as members of the political community and promotes their obligations as citizens by emphasizing the right and need to participate in decision-making in a broad range of democratic institutions. It appears to take the view that the citizen must participate in the democratic process in order to be a citizen. The central problem in all this is, of course, how to motivate young people to feel committed to democracy and convince them that it is in their interest to be so committed. Teachers will be inspected and judged on the extent to which they motivate the young in the collective interest. Schools will be required to devote 5 per cent of the National Curriculum to citizenship education by the year 2000 in order to achieve these learning outcomes. Schools will also have to decide how to teach children to be good citizens and select the content. The guiding principles on what citizenship is will be provided for them, which means teachers must comply with central government pronouncements on citizenship education.

However, attempts to select the content and agree the teaching strategies for citizenship education are likely to prove difficult, principally because there is no consensus about which teaching methods are best and which content will be the least controversial for citizenship education. Some research also indicates that citizenship education is largely ineffectual and that teachers are ill-equipped to meet these new demands. Another problem for teachers will be that it is not only cognitive knowledge that will be inspected. Teaching about loyalty and tolerance, for example, requires more than facts. Citizenship education is fundamentally concerned with moral education and it is also where education and politics meet. The Crick advisory group has set learning outcomes that are bound to involve affective learning outcomes, which are less objective and more difficult to measure and judge. We have already said that citizenship education involves instilling moral values, so yet another danger is that it may be used by moral relativists to instil scepticism in the young. Citizenship education requires careful examination in the light of the government's national promotion of it for it is certainly beset with problems and it might therefore be better for schools to focus their attention on strengthening their ethos as communities first. The implementation of citizenship education is an ambitious project since teachers will be faced with a set of learning outcomes, largely drawn up by academics, which may be impossible to achieve.

A communitarian perspective on citizenship education appears to focus on building a community in the school that places the greatest emphasis on responsibility coupled with corresponding rights. This communitarian approach does not stress those factors that differentiate individuals from each other and from the community, but rather stresses what they share with other individuals and what integrates them into the community. Radical individualism finds no place in such a community because the ethos of the school would strive to encourage a genuine human community where children are enabled to reach their full potential and where children feel that they belong. It will involve a group of people who share a common vision, common goals and common commitments. This within a context in which children learn to respect and accept each other despite differences and where there are equitable and open relations between teachers and pupils. This school community does not exist for itself, but for the service of others and the society beyond itself. It will require personal sacrifice and effort which are demanding of any individual. Without this basic background it is difficult to see how citizenship education can be anything other than an information advice course. Rhys Griffith (1998:33) describes two current approaches to citizenship education in the UK which he terms 'learning *about* citizenship' and 'learning *in* citizenship'. He says:

> Education about citizenship consists of teaching pupils about the rights and duties they will later have as citizens but do not presently have as pupils. Education in citizenship is child-centred and aims to develop citizenship through the child's exploration of her own rights and responsibilities via personal actions within the school community and environment.

While these two approaches are not necessarily discrete, the first approach demonstrates how citizenship education in schools can be reduced to offering basic information on rights and obligations which may, or may not, be acted upon by children.

The advisory group emphasized the involvement of pupils in participatory activities at school since it believed that this would help mould the character of children as citizens. Few schools involve their pupils in decision-making and therefore the possibility of acquiring practical knowledge of the processes which characterize civic and political life in the community are, at the present time, not open to the majority of pupils. Citizenship awareness does seem to be linked to active involvement by pupils in civic-like activities at school and is therefore a good precursor of civic commitment. The UNESCO international project on *What Education for What Citizenship* (1998) found a significant relationship between participation in school life and the wish to be involved later in the life of the community. The virtues of citizenship are intimately bound up with participation in community and the active promotion of the common good: a common good that leaves room for individual autonomy, but a definition which incorporates shared values. The advisory group specifically mentions the concern for the common good as one of the values and dispositions that children should learn in schools.

The Common Good

The 'common good' is a term of ancient origin and in contemporary usage it can be amorphous, meaning a variety of things. Its modern popularity can be measured by the fact that politicians of all political parties have employed it, for they all claim to work for the 'common good'. The majority of communitarians have adopted it as a central theme in their movement and by it they mean that individual citizens and voluntary groupings of individuals should make specific contributions to the common welfare of society. In so doing, these communitarians believe that individuals bring their own interests into harmony with the needs of the community. This, they claim, is done in accordance with the norms of justice and within the limits of the competence of each individual. Communitarians do not accept that individuals are totally self-interested or that they are separate or isolated from the communities in which they live. They also believe that individuals are prepared to associate with others in order to promote private interests which the whole community hold in common. However, the communitarian language used to describe the 'common good' is often problematic and a clearer definition of the term is required even if it cannot be answered definitively.

Aristotle believed that individuals can only function and realize their own ideals for life within a well-constructed and ordered polity. The purpose of classical education was namely the development of good citizens and education of individuals was guided by the aims and needs of the polity of which they are members. What is 'good' for the individual is ultimately fixed by what is 'good' for the polity. He says in *The Metaphysics*:

even if the good is the same for the individual and the state – the good of the state is clearly the greater and more perfect thing to attain and to preserve. It is something to obtain the good for one man alone; but to secure it for a nation and for a state is nobler and more divine.

(see McIntyre 1967)

However, he also says that it is the political context that will determine the good since, for Aristotle, ethics was closely related to politics; he described them as branches of the same discipline. For Aristotle, the focus of the study of politics is the common good which he says must have primacy. Plato also argued that what was good for the polity was by nature good for the individual and that the political community aims to achieve the common good of its members.

For both Aristotle and Aquinas 'community', or more accurately, 'communities' are the natural outgrowth of human flourishing. The family is the very basic unit of these communities and families nurture and educate their children and combine with other families into neighbourhoods which in turn become villages and towns and eventually a state and nation. Both believed that these communities would not function unless the individuals within them behaved ethically. To ensure the ethical behaviour in each community laws and an authority structure are required to administer necessary sanctions. The function of the State is to provide and maintain a framework in which its citizens can live 'the good life' – that is, achieve 'happiness'. This 'happiness' does not consist in some excessive bodily pleasures, but in the contemplation of truth and the possession of the virtue of wisdom. Therefore, one achieves happiness by living virtuously, which assumes sufficient material possessions to ensure good health and adequate leisure time. Aristotle saw this as the ideal of human perfection; he recognized that individuals would not be motivated to act towards this ideal in every case and that individuals would seek intermediate goods or lesser goods. The State therefore has a duty to teach these higher virtues to all its citizens.

Aquinas believed that the common good is greater than the individual and that it is rational for the individual to sacrifice some measure of his material goods and abilities for the sake of the community. He held the view that those who seek out the good of society also seek their own good because their own good cannot exist without the common good. However, Aquinas maintained that the common good cannot exist without justice, which in turn demands that the community respect and foster the well-being of all its members equally. The community cannot therefore arbitrarily sacrifice individuals to the common good. A community that allows this would forfeit its claim on the allegiance of its members. Indeed, Catholic teaching has consistently stated that the whole reason for the existence of civil authorities is the realization of the common good. This classical and Christian tradition of the common good points to a community of citizens committed to a common purpose because of the advantages it brings. They bond with each in association and promote the active membership of all citizens to share in the good life. Citizenship is concerned with the common good, some would say as the basis of the common good, and is defined as a good shared with others. The pursuit of the common good created by the community is for the benefit of all. This 'benefit of all' implies that there should be some distribution of the goods of society so that all have an interest in contributing to, as well as benefiting from, these goods.

Michael Novak (1989:176–7), a conservative thinker, employs a variant of the Thomistic view of the common good which distinguishes between the 'formal' and 'material' meaning of the term. The formal meaning refers to what is similar across all contexts while the material refers to the particular embodiments of the common good in any particular time or space. The formal aspect of the common good is dynamic – it moves towards the full and ultimate development of human beings by aiming to develop the personality of each individual in the most fully developed community of which they are capable. The material aspect refers to the common good that is attainable in any one time or place. Consequently, the common good is always 'under judgement' by a still higher standard, implicit in the fuller stage of human development yet to be achieved. As Novak (1989:177) says about the common good:

> The *formal* meaning points to the full (and future) conclusion of human development, both communal and personal. The *material* meaning points to the existing level of human development already achieved at any one point in time or space, or as the next proximate level of development that in practice may be realized.

Therefore, in Novak's view, the common good at each level of concrete achievement recognizes both an end achieved and a new inward impulse towards further development.

An immediate observation about the material meaning of the

common good is that it is open to numerous and often contradictory political opinions. The realities suggested by the material content of the common good include: the provision of public transport; public health and education; public recreation and park areas; public care programmes for both young and elderly; public security and law; and much more besides. Arguments about how these should be provided for the common good of society abound in modern politics. Consequently, effective citizens must participate in achieving the common good through the democratic process. It is why it is easier to encourage people to pursue the formal meaning of the common good than to figure out, in practice, which of the many material courses of action will best attain it. The *formal* common good is what is intended by the person of good will because they are open to the good, and desire it and pursue it even before knowing what, materially, the good is. The good citizen therefore intends the common good of their society, but cannot foresee the concrete shape that such a common good will take. It is also why Bellah concludes that:

> if we avoid any utopian expectations, I believe that it is still important to talk about the common good or even about the good society. We need a standard to measure where we are, even if we cannot expect to live up to it any time soon.
>
> (quoted in Novak 1989:111)

This appears to suggest that if we aim at the ideal we can achieve something good. Despite this, we are left with a multiplicity of purposes that the common good is intended to accomplish.

In this view the common good does not require that individuals suppress their individual interests, only that they adjust their actions so as to be compatible with and to promote the development of the capacities of others. Common interests can be achieved without having to set aside your own interests. It is even possible that self-interest can have a transformative power and materially assist the common good. The common good includes two essential aspects, which are inseparable: the development of the capacities and powers of unique and irreplaceable human beings and the development of cooperative, fraternal, and mutually helpful ways of associating. In other words, individual growth means the widening and expanding of one's horizons to include others and their concerns. Nevertheless, there are some who cannot agree that abortion and euthanasia promote the common good and may even decide that as citizens they cannot obey a law if it seriously injures their idea of the good. This may result in some groups placing their interests before other groups in society, but their aim is to benefit society by providing what they perceive to be 'good' for the people. In other words, there exists for them a collective or public interest that can be promoted by individuals, voluntary intermediate organizations, and government for the sake of the 'common good' of society. A 'thick' communitarian perspective on the common good would hold that the common good is common to the community as a whole and to each member and that the common good and community are constitutive of the good of each member. Further, that the good of each individual is realizable within the context of the community and that the common good functions as an objective standard by which the choices of each individual are evaluated.

In contemporary society individuals have very different life choices so how can they have a common aim? Some have claimed that individuals alone are best placed to judge what is good for them. Therefore, is the 'common good' consistent with personal liberties? Liberals often argue that it is best to promote practical cooperation among individuals rather than common purposes; indeed, that within a pluralistic society it is impossible to have a common good, only different opinions of what is good. They ask if it is really the case that what is good for the individual is good for society? Liberals also make the obvious point that we cannot know with certainty what the common good is in any particular case since the common good is really part of the contested nature of politics itself. This liberal attack on the notion of the common good undermines the position adopted by many communitarians who believe that the common good is relatively knowable. There is also conflict between private and public goods and so there obviously needs to be some kind of a balance, which is why John Gray (1994:1) argues that the State should be limited in its government. He says this is an ethical argument and notes that:

> The scope of government authority in Britain remains vastly overextended. The autonomous institutions of civil society are today threatened by an invasive State whose size and arbitrary power have not substantially diminished, and in important respects have been enhanced.

He specifically details education as one of those areas where the State has over extended its authority in recent years. No doubt the government would claim that its education policies were for the common good. A number of New Right theorists would extend Gray's observations and argue that the government should provide only those goods which all need and which cannot be supplied by markets. In this view it is the market that distributes the goods of society through fair competition. Every individual competes for the limited resources of society and the State simply ensures a set of rules so that no one has an unfair advantage. Achievement of the common good is therefore reached by means of the voluntary cooperation of self-interested individuals. Richard Epstein (1998:150) argues that communitarian rhetoric presupposes that individuals will go along with activities that satisfy some idea of the common good even at the cost of some personal dislocation. He rejects this communitarian view and believes instead that (p. 4):

> we must justify any statements about the collective interest solely by how it advances the individual welfare of each and every citizen, be he friend or foe, popular or despised. So understood, their happiness, their pains, their successes, and their emotions matter; what is irrelevant, and dangerous, is some distant conception of the public good that is not anchored to the utility of any human being and that disregards the separateness of persons.

Epstein is a strong defender of limited government for he believes that State involvement in social institutions should be limited. He seeks to promote the reconciliation of individual liberty with the common good, but principally through a free market of social relations.

Bill Jordan (1989) believes that this line of thinking can replace the notion of a public morality with a combination of commercial relations and private morality. The State no longer promotes a public morality among its citizens in order for them to promote the common good, and citizenship itself is separated from public morality. Instead citizens pursue their own competitive advantage. Appeals to the common good in this situation could be interpreted as appeals to individuals to act against their own interests. Jordan (1989:85) describes a number of characteristics of the common good that contrast with this market view and that fit well with many communitarian versions of the concept. First, he says that the common good is created by citizens participating together in some shared process. Second, the common good is not susceptible to quantitative division, but is entirely qualitative. Third, the common good is purposeful, which means that achieving it must be adapted over time. Fourth, the common good requires power to be used to structure interests and distribute assets, so as to create conditions for active participation and self-rule. However, this power must not be used to further the interests of individuals and groups for this corrupts society and destroys the common good. In such a situation the State would be unworthy of loyalty because the common good is being exploited by dominant groups.

Many communitarians appear, at first sight, to be followers of the Aristotle/Aquinas line for many of their postulates are rooted in ancient and medieval philosophies which in turn are interwoven with contemporary thought. Etzioni (1998:91) has commented that communitarians 'have championed the concept of the common good and pointed to the limitations of relying only on the good as individually formulated'. He gives the title of *Rights and the Common Good* (1995c) to one of his edited collections even when it generally ignores discussion of the concept itself. However, there appears to be a tension in Etzioni's thought between both social virtues and individual rights. Etzioni is very sensitive to any accusation that he is a majoritarian or a social conservative. While rejecting the liberal view, which holds that it is for individuals to formulate their own 'good' and 'virtues' and that these cannot be taught, he also rejects the conservative view, which holds that the 'common good' exists independently of the individual and should be taught by the State. Etzioni adopts a middle course which states that it is through a respect for authentic autonomy and for persuasion and education that we can promote the idea of the common good. For Etzioni the virtues within the concept of the 'common good' are limited to some core values – which is really his device for excluding issues such as abortion and instead justifying safety devices in cars as promoting part of the common good. His concept of the common good, in fact, does not follow the Aristotle/Aquinas line but is instead an even more idealistic form of contemporary liberal arguments. He concludes (1998:257):

> In short, a person should hold on to the values he or she finds most compelling, seeking to be joined by the community but steadfast even if others initially or ultimately do not approve. The community provides one with a normative foundation, a starting point, culture and tradition, fellowship, and place for moral dialogue, but is not the ultimate moral arbitrator. The members are.

The implications for education are that society needs to teach a set of values that can be accepted and shared in society in order to formulate its public policy. Therefore it follows that citizenship education should be taught as part of a more flexible National Curriculum. The framework for Etzioni is that the common good is a guide to individual action; it can be changed by society. Etzioni also avoids defining what the common good consists of, except by providing some obvious examples. His ideas make the concept of the common good even more confused and amorphous. His liberal use of the terms conscience, autonomy and community make for even more contradictions and render the common good an unendingly contestable term. Nevertheless, the general communitarian focus on the 'common good' and citizenship have implications for schools as civic institutions.

Schools as Civic Institutions

A great deal of communitarian language uses both the 'common good' and 'virtue' to promote the ideal of the community. This view suggests that if we are to know the good we must be educated in virtue. We need to grow within a community with a distinctive tradition that is taught to all its members. Today, many communitarians claim that we lack a conception of the good because of modern pluralism and therefore we need to focus on virtues in small communities and learn them in order to share a vision of the human good again, and that in schools each person needs to be treated as an autonomous individual while at the same time part of the community. Yet it is extremely complex to include within the common good respect for diversity among persons. The common good is larger than any individual, but not complete in itself. The common good, some would argue, must be constructed through discussion, it should be forged not found. Schools can contribute to this process by encouraging decision-making within shared debates over issues such as justice and freedom. In schools common interests can be promoted and created and fostered through active citizenship. Schools can reward cooperative acts by individuals and praise those who serve the common good while condemning selfish behaviour. Many schools in Britain already implement this as part of what they see as a liberal education, which is understood as the education of the well-informed citizen. A number of schools also provide an education focused on good citizenship that appeals directly to the public spirit of individuals, encouraging them to take pleasure in working towards collective ends. Communitarians believe that many more schools should follow this path and should reassert the claims of common over private interests, and public participation over private duty.

The attempt to reconstruct interest in the common good is a difficult task but the greater emphasis now given to the concept of virtues in education has the potential to assist this process. On both the political right and left there has been a revival of virtues based on tradition and particularity – a movement from values to virtues. Values can be whatever any individual or group happens to value, at any time, for any reason. Values in education often claim moral equality and neutrality and individuals are expected to be non-judgemental about values, for people today generally accept that any one's values are as good as the next person's – values are certainly broader than virtues. In contrast, we cannot say that any one's virtues are the same as the next person's. Communitarians would argue that education and schooling have a definite role in the adequate preparation for discharging the duties and responsibilities of citizenship through the cultivation of appropriate virtues. These virtues are habits of action or rather acting with due restraint on one's impulses, having regard for the rights of others. Virtues are not learnt through values analysis or clarification teaching in school, but by regular repetition of right actions, however small these actions are. Virtues are therefore settled dispositions or traits of character formed by and necessary to sustain a lifetime of thought and good actions. Communitarians have recognized that an increasing number of philosophers and educationalists think that a focus on virtues can form the basis of morality, but often then reduce this virtue-based morality to simply rhetoric that encourages conscientious adherence to duty among young people in schools. In contrast, Brian Wilcox (1997:259), commenting on the philosophy of Alasdair McIntyre says:

> McIntyre seeks the restoration of an essentially Aristotelian approach in which an education in the virtues has a central place; in which my good as a person is one and the same as that of others in the human community of which I am a member. The exercise of the virtues is a necessary and central *part* of the good life and not simply a *means* to achieve such a life ... in contemporary individualist morality the virtues have been displaced from their former central position. In their stead are rules which aspire to universality. Virtues, in so far as the term is used at all, are seen simply as dispositions necessary to produce obedience to the rules.

Nevertheless, for many communitarians the school remains a community devoted to learning and its citizens are teachers and pupils who should be engaged in virtue-building educational activities. Bentley (1998:65) usefully reminds us that:

> Virtue, the exercise of character and the practice of ethical conduct, is built out of experience rather than intellect as a set of rules or abstract values, and, as Aristotle pointed out, such experience comes from active participation in the rules and norms governing an institution or a community.

While citizenship education is part of a liberal education, we need to ask what are the standards by which we judge whether a pupil is politically competent? Robert Dahl (1995) provides educators with a communitarian way of understanding the modern citizen. First, he speaks of the *good citizen* who knows the common good and desires to pursue it. This type of citizen seeks the good of some larger collectivity of which he is part by seeking the good of all, the general good, the public interest. He is well informed about public affairs and political issues and is strongly motivated to foster the common good. Second, *the self-interested citizen* seeks only the good of himself and perhaps his family and friends. They may have knowledge of the common good but have no incentive to pursue it. Indeed, he has more incentive to understand his own interests and when there is a conflict between these interests and those of the community he opts for his own self-interest. Few citizens in Western democracies measure up to Dahl's first view of the citizen, but few are as totally egotistical as the second view. Dahl believes that both these views are unsatisfactory as a description of the average citizen. Dahl proposes a third view which is of the *adequate citizen* who knows something of political affairs and participates in a minimal way in public and civic activities. However, even here Dahl believes that modern societies do not produce *adequate citizens* in sufficient number, since only a small minority of citizens are interested in politics and fewer still are engaged in political life, so he calls for us to raise citizen competence through education. He recognizes that more information about democracy does not necessarily lead to greater competence or heightened understanding among citizens.

An education for citizenship, or the promotion of the common good, needs, therefore, to encourage practices of cooperation, friendship, openness and active participation in society. Schools do not impose their definition of the common good but provide opportunities for pupils to experience the reality of these practices. Pupils do not know the common good innately but must learn how subtle a concept it is and to realize that the material content of the common good at one point in time is the most disputatious of subjects. It should set off a number of discussions, not settle the argument. The implications for schools is that shared debates and shared discussions should be encouraged. One way to facilitate this is the establishment of school councils which the advisory group on citizenship strongly recommended. The advisory group believed that the preparation for active citizenship can be helped or hindered by the ethos and organization of a school. The group encouraged schools to provide opportunities for pupils to exercise responsibility and initiatives and for schools to consult with pupils where their opinions can prove relevant both to the efficient running of the school and to the general motivation for learning. The group itself stopped short of recommending compulsory school councils and community service as integral parts of citizenship education. In contrast Rhys Griffith (1998:35) argues against school councils on the basis that they deny citizenship opportunities to the majority by taking away direct decision-making on the part of the individual.

A communitarian view might seek to establish democratic structures in schools with pupils involved in decision-making. This would involve election of pupils to councils and committees; a pupils' charter of rights; a grievance procedure; pupils setting the school standard of dress through their council; and clear responsibilities and obligations discussed with the teachers. Teachers would also be expected to have a vote on matters within the school and operate within teams and working parties. They would seek a real partnership with parents. By seeking a more democratic structure for schools citizenship can be lived and practised, but the communal school will also pursue shared values and activities that encourage a commitment to the common good. While citizenship education could be used to transform society and the social structures the common good might serve as counterbalance to much of the prevailing individualism of modern society. Henry Tam (1998), with his own unique but problematic vision of communitarianism, believes that we need to build inclusive communities, but that first we should develop citizens who can participate in 'co-operative enquiry'. This 'co-operative enquiry' he defines as claims to truth being judged valid only if informed participants deliberating together under conditions of cooperative enquiry accept the claim to be true. This suggests that there are no truths, only interpretations. Tam (1998:249) concludes that:

> In terms of education, support must be given to develop students'
> abilities to assess the validity of knowledge claims; teach them to
> reflect on the nature of their common values, and acquire a habit
> of acting responsibly; and introduce them to sharing and exercising
> power with others for the common good.

His explanation for his own claims remain elusive, but he is effectively
calling for a transformation of current attitudes and conditions within
society without spelling out exactly where this change leads. For him,
'communitarian citizenship' is about learning to become a member of
an inclusive community and participating within this community as
an equal in determining how decisions affecting oneself are made.

Conclusion

Citizenship education is a concept that can only be understood within
the political and social context and historical tradition in which it has
been developed. In Britain today the context is one of extensive constitutional change from incorporating European Human Rights to the
reform of the House of Lords. It is also a context in which the British
have a less developed sense of citizenship than practically any other
European country. Citizenship education is also an educational aim of
the State, with its principal purpose being the preservation of the State.
Consequently, citizenship education is expected to display a range of
pro-social attitudes and is the reason why there is always a behavioural
component woven into its aims and purposes. Communitarians have
been successful in appealing for more citizenship education because
many within society dislike the perceived individualism and indifference amongst citizens towards their fellows. New Labour is making
more explicit the moral rationale behind the school curriculum. The
government wants to produce women and men who have the character
and competence to be supportive of democratic government. This goal
is by no means new, but communitarians are giving first emphasis to
the civic, moral, social and political obligations of citizens as a way of
combating individualism and indifference. However, New Labour does
not appear to have a fully worked out agenda for citizenship and moral
education. Tom Bentley (1998:66) may help with his summary of
these contested concepts:

> So, learning to be a moral agent, and to be a citizen, begins in the
> family and the school. But surely citizenship extends beyond these

institutions? The goal of citizenship education is to enable young people to develop into active responsible citizens in the wider world. Schools are the institutions which contain a young person's activity for most of their first two decades, but they also live in the wider world; they are members of numerous communities, and their expectations and sources of learning are far richer and more diverse than school-based learning opportunities, however good these might be. As young people grow into the wider world, it is appropriate to seek opportunities to extend their problem-solving abilities, their concern for others, and their exercise of ethical conduct beyond the school gates.

He uses the work of the National Forum on Values in Education and the Community to illustrate how citizenship education begins with the *self* and then radiates outward through personal *relationships* to communities, and finally to *society*. For Bentley (1998:64–5) there is at each stage a series of learning experiences which are necessary for children to find their role in the community. The central question remains unanswered: why do some people participate and others do not?

For most people there are also intractable difficulties and a lack of consensus with the concept of the common good. Communitarians seem to suggest that the common good can be determined by widespread political and civic participation and through extensive discussion and reasoned debate by well-prepared and educated citizens. This argument is disputed and challenged by liberals such as Linda Raeder (1989) who comments that:

> All we can truly have in common with our fellows in a great society [Western societies], and thus the only basis for a genuine agreement regarding the common good, are certain shared *abstract* values and opinions regarding the 'kind of society' in which we would like to live, as opposed to opinions about the particular manifestations it should assume. Commitment to such shared general values, not the pursuit of common concrete purposes, constitutes social cohesion in a great society. No one can possess the concrete knowledge required to justify a rational pursuit of common concrete ends. The common knowledge we do possess is confined to certain *abstract* features of our social and physical environment (we share knowledge of the *kind* of clothing we wear, the *kind* of food we eat, the *kind* of literature we enjoy, and so on). Most of the innumerable and ever-changing facts and circumstances that determine the

concrete shape of our fellows' lives in the spatially extensive contemporary liberal order are and must forever remain unknown to us.

Therefore, according to this view no amount of discussion or deliberation by well-informed citizens can produce agreement on the particular concrete manifestations of the common good. Nevertheless, communitarians generally believe that there is an essential correspondence between the character of the citizen and the common good of the community. Ultimately, if a citizen does not care about others or the common good then there is little likelihood that he or she will become constructively engaged in civic life. It is also important to stress again that while communitarianism is interested in schooling it also equally addresses other educating institutions such as the family and organized religion.

5 Communitarianism and Religiously Affiliated Schools

> What marks such a [constitutive] community is not a spirit of benevolence or the prevalence of communitarian values, or even certain 'shared final ends' alone, but a common vocabulary of discourse and a background of implicit practices and understandings.
>
> (Michael Sandel, *Liberalism and the Limits of Justice* 1982)

It is interesting to note that, at face value, many of the arguments for a communitarian public philosophy ideal of the community fit extremely well with many of the shared practices within religiously affiliated schools. Buddhism, Christianity, Hinduism, Islam, Judaism, and Sikhism place strong emphasis on the communal nature of human existence and they teach that we find our identity and selves, in substantial part, in relationship with others. They also have a keen sense of history and a desire for continuity and tradition which Robert Bellah (1985), as we have seen already, terms 'a community of memory'. All these religions emphasize community, solidarity and very specific duties and rights among their members. All respect tradition, sacred texts and are concerned with the supernatural. All believe, to varying degrees, that education begins with parents in the home and that the whole curriculum in the school should be set to reflect their particular beliefs and be supplementary to the home. The communal elements and characteristics of all these religions would therefore permeate the content and process of the education provided in such religiously affiliated schools and would help form the identity and values of individuals within these school communities – but only partly by individuals being together and sharing time and experiences. These experiences would necessarily consist of prayer and worship within a faith community, but would also include social dimensions with individuals encouraged in various degrees to participate in and with the wider

95

community or society. All these religions are not monolithic systems of religious belief, since there are considerable differences within them, but they each represent a distinctive 'community of memory'.

In Western culture, Christianity has played a central role in forming the social practices of communities. It has also engaged with many of the central themes in communitarianism throughout history. An Anglican conference in Oxford in July 1937 on the 'Church, Community and the State' discussed a number of these central communitarian themes. The conference members were concerned that the selfish individualism that they saw in American and British societies of the 1930s would end in anarchy and the dissolution of society itself. They concluded that individualism, or 'free personality', was the main aim of many education programmes and that this was harmful, not only to society, but to the individual themselves. They felt that, while the sharing of a history, a common home and social practices, and a common life in time and space constituted a community, to rely on the rights afforded by the laws of any particular society rendered the individual insecure. This conference identified many of the key elements on the communitarian agenda today and clearly demonstrates that there appear to be many points of contact between communitarianism and Christianity. There are also points of contact between communitarianism and Judaism, as can be seen from Jonathan Sacks' book *The Politics of Hope*. As the Chief Rabbi in Britain, he endorsed communitarianism as a public philosophy defined as an attempt to bridge the gap between the State and the individual.

In order to illustrate the many points of contact between communitarianism and religion this chapter will look at one particular Christian religious tradition in education represented here by the Catholic Church, but the chapter will also refer to other religious traditions. The reasons for focusing on Catholic schools are essentially three-fold. First, there is generally a greater amount of recent research data on Catholic schools. Second, the connection between the Church's social thinking and education is more explicitly stated in Catholicism. Third, a number of academics believe that aspects of communitarianism have emerged from Catholicism (Paul Vallely 1998). It is true that the Catholic Church has a very distinctive social teaching that has much in common with aspects of communitarian thinking, but it is important to state at the outset that it is not the same. Much of this common thinking between Catholicism and communitarianism predates the latter, as can be seen from Kenneth Grasso's (1996) collection of essays on *Catholicism, Liberalism and Communitarianism*. Catholicism has a very strong intellectual tradition that offers a number of challenges to both communitarianism and liberalism. Catholicism shares communitarian concerns about society, especially the selfishness and materialism manifested by radical individualism and the fact that local communities are beset by ever-increasing State power. There are indeed many surface similarities between Catholicism and communitarianism as a public philosophy which have attracted Catholics to it, but we need to look behind these similarities. Like liberalism, many of the versions of communitarianism do not offer any transcendent moral vision against which all individuals are held accountable. Many in the communitarian movement reject the reverence for religious tradition and supernatural standards and distrust religious principles because they feel that such principles are often intolerant to other individuals pursuing alternative lifestyles. This is certainly the case with New Labour. The communitarian movement's first commitment is to public service and democracy and in this it shares much with liberalism, including the notion that traditional religious practices prevent us from pursuing our own ends and are therefore oppressive. Weaker versions of communitarianism seek in the company of liberalism the freedom of the individual to make their own decisions. Therefore, these communitarians are really liberals who wish to establish a particular common sense among the people in an effort to create a shared sense of political identity and purpose. There appears to be nothing in this liberalized form of communitarianism that differs fundamentally from liberalism. What then is a (weaker) communitarian understanding of the role of religion in this scheme of things?

Civic Religion

As has been said, most forms of liberalism have always sought the exclusion of religion from influence on public policy on the grounds that religion encourages oppression of the individual. Religion teaches that service to one's neighbour is more important than increasing one's enjoyment and it also encourages people to follow the will of others or God rather than their own. Religion is therefore dangerous in the liberal mind set. Some forms of communitarianism appear to be more sympathetic towards religion, advocating that we should listen and take seriously the religious voice in public policy discourse and some of them support many of the social aspects of religious practice, including the strengthening of the family. Communitarians such as Robert Bellah (1991) argue that religion is a crucial element in public life, while William Galston (1991) and Charles Taylor (1989) believe that religion should be allowed into public debate in society. However, this must not blind religious individuals to the real intention of these communitarian thinkers. Many communitarians confine the function of religion to its instrumental purposes in supporting democratic society and see religion as only a part of the life of the community and as merely one option among many. While they support the family, it is because they believe that the family reproduces the habits and virtues essential for the maintenance of liberal democracy. While they also support character-forming institutions like schools, these are seen as being necessary for the 'good' life and religion is therefore judged by its political consequences in producing 'good' citizens. Bellah believes that religion is only useful if it promotes egalitarian community. In other words, if religion supports his particular version of social justice then it may be judged useful in his eyes. Galston judges religion's worth in the measure of support it lends to a liberal community, but he would not allow religion to play a part in determining the sex roles of individuals within a democracy since this, he claims, would foster dissension and intolerance. Many communitarians also see no truth in religion *per se*; they reject natural law and the authority of religious custom and consider aspects of Catholicism in particular to be both authoritarian and oppressive of individual growth. As Brian Mitchell (1995) says:

> Christian Communitarians typically downplay the Christian aspect of their outlook, often making a great show of their 'sensitivity' to non-Christians. They do not evangelize on behalf of Christianity, but on behalf of 'Western culture' or 'Judaeo-Christian values'. They appeal more often to a rationalized, desanctified, nonsectarian Natural Law than to divine revelation or Tradition, both of which are sect specific and thus 'divisive', 'exclusive', and potentially 'offensive'. Of course, the least desire of Communitarians is to divide the community. Above all, they want unity, based upon shared interests, and they naturally seek the lowest common denominator to obtain it.

Bellah and Galston are really advocating a 'civic religion', for as Galston (1991:221) says: 'We must found a civil religion that will make us teach virtue to our young, not in the name of God, but in the name of the nation and its people'. This would entail making sacred political ideals and perhaps even giving first place to patriotism.

This type of communitarian-inspired civic religion appears to have much in common with National Socialism and the worship of the State. The significant idea here is the primacy of the people over the individual. It stresses cooperation between the national government and big business for the betterment of the nation as a whole and therefore easily accommodates the communitarian and New Labour idea of a free economy tempered with a strong communal outlook. This 'communal outlook' does not rest on the notions of class affiliation, but on the idea that we are part of 'one nation, one community'. As Driver and Martell say:

> Communitarian thinking usually asserts that questions of value and justice are essentially local because they are embedded in, and relative to, particular communities. The 'local' to New Labour is the United Kingdom. Yet New Labour has opted for moral values that transcend communities within the UK.

Bruce Frohnen (1996) observes that this civic religion is more to do with what is required by the nation than by God, more to do with law and order than with salvation and love. The purpose of religion in this view is purely terrestrial because there is no transcendent sphere available to human beings. It is everything to do with glorifying individuals. Individual conduct in this model of society would be regulated by the standards of the nation that are derived from the shared values in the common memory of a nation's history. Dale Snauwaert (1995) provides a communitarian interpretation of this when he says:

> From this perspective, the rights and duties of citizenship are founded upon a political morality demarcated by national sovereignty, for if rights and duties are derived from the political and moral authority inherent in the community, and no higher authority exists, then citizenship and civic education must be premised upon the sovereignty of the community. If the community is conceived as being national, then citizenship is demarcated by the nation. Thus, a national civic education is contingent upon the imperatives of the political morality inherent in the national political culture, its politeia.

This understanding of civic education ignores the internationalism that Catholic, Jewish and Islamic education offer for extending the individual's self-identification beyond the national community.

Bellah views religion as political and he praises mainline Protestantism as being valuable because of the shared moral values it inculcates in individuals. He believes that morality comes through participation in democratic life and that religion (mainly Protestant religion) is an indispensable requirement for government in providing a firm moral consensus for the community. This is a good example of how many communitarians look back, implicitly or explicitly, to the Protestant tradition that has shaped modern America. The purpose of this civic religion is to form us into a community or nation through civil religious symbolism. Bellah would argue that national monuments, patriotic holiday observations and political rhetoric in America provide us with an example of this civic religion. This secular religion uses the secular practices and myths of society to build individuals together and observance of these patriotic rituals becomes its liturgy. It is these ceremonies and symbols that allow Americans to explain their experiences, as Americans, to themselves. Again, there is nothing new in these communitarian ideas. In the *Declaration of the Rights of Man and the Citizen*, published in 1792, Thomas Paine promulgated a number of 'sacred rights' and through these effectively advocated a civic religion. Rousseau also thought a civic religion was necessary and while the philosophy of both Paine and Rousseau relied on the notion of a God or Supreme Being, it was not the Christian God. In the same way the American Declaration of Independence moved in the direction of religion, but it is a theology that gives priority to what human beings want. Bruce Frohnen (1992) believes that for Robert Bellah religion's utility derives from its promotion of public morality and political virtue. It is not surprising, therefore, that the national civic celebrations and commemorative holidays in the USA have largely displaced religious festivals, as they did during the French Revolution.

Garry Wills (1990), another public philosophy communitarian, attempts to reconstruct religion by urging us to constantly rethink and recreate our society on a regular basis. He argues that the Catholic Church must compromise and allow abortion, divorce, contraception, married priests, women priests, etc. He believes that the Catholic Church must please its constituents in order to lead them and through this win a place in the public policy debate. Merging religion and politics clearly appears to be the aim of these communitarians. Etzioni (1997:254–5) also adopts this secular approach to religion, for he says that religious people must balance their specifically religious views with respect for individual autonomy, especially the rights of others, by limiting the scope of their idea of the good to 'core values'. No indication of what these 'core values' might be are given and he also warns us to be aware of 'puritan' religious absolutes without telling us what religious views he has in mind.

This secular communitarian view shares much with Paul Hirst, an influential educationalist in England in the 1970s, who denied the very possibility of constructing a useful relationship between Christian faith and education. Indeed, he went so far as to say that Christianity had no contribution to make to an understanding of education and that it would be illegitimate to apply it in this way. Hirst distinguishes between two concepts of education: primitive and objective. The former is concerned with passing on customs and rituals while the latter is concerned with truth and reason. For Hirst the primitive idea of education cannot be recognized as 'education' at all. He says that when it comes to rational, sophisticated education 'dominated by a concern for knowledge, for truth and for reason' there can be no such thing as Christian education. However, Hirst seeks an accommodation with the individual Christian, but exclusively on his own terms. He suggests that his view of education should be acceptable to the Christian who adopts a rationally coherent system of thinking about education by beginning with basic premises that are self-evident to reason. Here Hirst is accusing Christians of irrationality, for the Christian whom Hirst has in mind is presumably one who will accept his view of education insofar as he is 'intelligent' and not insofar as he is a Christian. Hirst's idea of a Christian is contrary to the Christian view since Christianity claims to pursue a rational wholeness and does not accept an argument that seeks to combine intelligible with unintelligible beliefs. The Christian who accepts Hirst's position is accepting his or her irrationality or, by insisting that religious belief does have something to contribute to education, refuses to go along with this totally secularist position. The thrust of Hirst's arguments is towards the irrelevancy of religious beliefs, especially dogmatic Catholicism, for an understanding of education. Public philosophy communitarians invite Catholics to do exactly the same by adopting a purely ethical and democratic view of religion.

Bruce Frohnen (1996:80) observes that the logic of this argument dictates that:

> The church must abandon its commitment to moral absolutes. Indeed, there are no moral absolutes because a moral rule's unpopularity renders it invalid. Of course, this raises public opinion to the status of a moral absolute. It makes it morally wrong to

enforce an unpopular rule. By enforcing rules its members do not like, in Will's view, the church rejects political compromise (and good leadership) with its constituents in favour of prideful insistence on unobtainable goals.

Frohnen is very critical of communitarian approaches to religion and believes that an individual character is formed mainly through belief in God, parental authority and tradition. He suggests that some communitarians ascribe meaning to community and other words which do not have the power they give to them, and he believes that the meaning of life requires transcendence and salvation, which are the ultimate goals of life. Essentially, most communitarian notions of religion are more ethical than religious, more secular than spiritual, and more to do with certain standards of democratic conduct than to do with an individual's relationship with God, or indeed God's relationship with him or her. These communitarians see religion, particularly Protestantism, as presenting a set of moral principles that are useful as a means of rehabilitating national political life. By attempting to integrate their understanding of religion into their political programmes they render religion meaningless. Public philosophy communitarians appear to use the word God frequently, as do many other politicians in America, but their use of the word has a bewildering ambiguity about it. We can, therefore, conclude that the origins of this communitarian ideal of religion is more Greek than Christian because in the Greek city-state religious, moral and political authority were homogeneous. A Catholic wishing to be a committed public philosophy communitarian must concede that the derived outcomes of Christian ethics can be achieved without Christian doctrine, and that, in fact, in the public policy domain, doctrine may well militate against the possibility of the desired social outcomes. Christians are effectively being asked to support a public morality that all reasonable citizens, whether religious or non-religious, could come to agree on, independent of their own particular moral and religious views. However, the notion of Catholic or Islamic morality suggests that certain things, like abortion, should not be tolerated, no matter how sincerely someone may feel that his or her actions are an intrinsic part of their conception of the good. The price of agreement between many communitarians and religious people must therefore be vacuity. How then can this communitarianism contribute anything useful to the public understanding of the religious school?

Towards a Religious Communitarian View?

Alasdair McIntyre, as a more traditional communitarian theorist, indicates that local communities need to foster the traditions and practices that produce Christian virtues. These virtues are not the result of some rational discourse among individuals, but are rather the product of a religious tradition embedded within a particular faith community and woven into the stories that this faith community tells about itself and its saints. McIntyre believes that the Christian narrative provides a clear end and a strong conception of the human good. A Catholic school, as an extension of the Church, is one of these 'local communities' with a clear purpose. McIntyre (1988) believes that these traditions and practices can only manifest their rationality through encounter and confrontation with rivals. Clearly, then, these traditions and practices are distinctive and a Catholic school may find its expressions of 'rationality' questioned or even dismissed by secular educationalists, including some types of communitarians. As part of the wider Catholic community, the Catholic school seeks to place a high priority on learning and appropriating the traditions, texts, practices and *mores* of Catholic life. In this way the Catholic school can lead its pupils to a virtuous life and help them attain the good life. McIntyre therefore reaffirms tradition and religion in the formation of individuals. Clearly McIntyre encourages us to think on a community of traditional practices that make for excellence of character. It is why Michael Golby (1997) concludes that only religious schools are communities of memory that can accommodate the basic communitarian aims in education.

This line of thought is often criticized or seen as moralistic élitism, but Catholic schools have traditionally focused on encouraging a sense of obligation among their pupils, with the emphasis on what the pupils can do to maintain the community and less on what the community can do for them. Pupils in Catholic schools are encouraged to practice traditional obligations that are found in the Catholic faith and Catholic educators have long believed that responsibility must be taught. As Cochran (1989) says: 'Acceptance of authority, loyalty to ideals and commitment to an historical community, though they do require sacrifice and closure of options, are the very stuff of character building'. Cochran believes that communitarians do not take seriously these essential elements of authority, loyalty and commitment. Many religious schools seek to address these concepts and encourage a real sense of belonging through membership of a community with shared values and beliefs that help create a sense of solidarity and unity coupled with shared commitment. This view of Catholic education is perhaps best described by Bryk et al. (1993:54) when they said:

> The dignity of the person rooted in community is also affirmed. Through immersion in Catholic religious tradition, the school seeks to develop students' views of life aims to be pursued. Through sharing a common life infused with the symbols and rituals of community, hope for the future, and active commitment towards humanity and social solidarity are encouraged.

Parents send their children to Catholic schools voluntarily; in choosing a Catholic school they signify a willingness to join a particular community and to accept its shared practices. In selecting an Islamic school for their children Muslim parents are expressing the same view of education, as Manzoor-ul-Hague (1993) says:

> Individuals possess potentialities, but these can be actualized only in a favourable social milieu and through co-operation with congenial companions. Membership of a group held together by mutual sympathy and understanding and inspired by a high ideal is the guarantee of self-development.

Bryk et al. (1993:28ff) claim that the educational provision within Catholic schools is embedded within an organization of the school as a community that has three core features. First, there are numerous school activities that encourage high levels of participation and provide for interactions among teachers and students. These activities would include residential retreats, school worship, athletics and drama. Second, teachers are not simply concerned about the transmission of knowledge, but are involved with students outside the classroom and often with their families. Research by James Coleman et al. (1987) found that Catholic schools in the USA were providing a better education than the public schools. The reason was that pupils in Catholic schools were receiving more support from their families and from the Church. The Catholic school was the extension of the family and of the ecclesial community of which that family is a part. Public schools, by contrast, represented the impersonal forces of both the government and the market more than the values of families. Catholic schools are an exception to this trend because they represent the values of the family and Church. Catholic schools in Britain are also academically successful and they confirm that a distinctive ethos with clear expectations of conduct contribute to the effective school. Third, there are a set of shared beliefs about what students should learn that gives meaning to much of the daily lives of both teachers and students. They conclude by saying that the Catholic school is a voluntary community and it is precisely because of this voluntary element that it is different from public schools. It is this voluntary commitment to the Catholic school which creates a community that is inescapably value-laden, for it is not something that just happens, it is something that is worked at. Therefore, it is not enough for teachers and pupils to be together, they must be tied together by a shared interest which has some degree of endurance over time. In this way the community becomes intrinsically educative. The Catholic idea of community means that all members of the Church are called to participate in the education of community members for there is a learning function in the very decision of commitment to be within any community. In regard to the Catholic school, the term community is used constantly to convey the notion that there should be a consensus of aims and values and mutually supportive relationships. The unity within a Catholic school community is inherently consensual since the source of oneness is entirely a matter of conviction. This raises the question of whether non-Catholics can be full members of a 'community of faith' that can often seem dogmatic and insular to those outside.

Thomas Groome (1996:116) makes the point that the Catholic school should be both a 'public community' and an 'ecclesial community'. The public aspect of this community would contribute to the common good and to the promotion of a social responsibility that is against individualism and social indifference. The purpose of Catholic education is to encourage students to care about and contribute to the common good and to be concerned for the marginalized within society. As he says:

> Commitment to community advises a pedagogy grounded in relationship, and marked by participation, by conversation and cooperation...formation in a social consciousness calls for teaching styles that encourage critical reflection and questioning of the social/political context, that nurture creative imagination about what can and should be done in the public arena.

However, Catholic schools do not always follow this model and Alan McClelland (1991:173) comments that:

The weakness of the Catholic school, however, has often been its inability to establish a confident internal polity that eschews that element of divisiveness inherent in the attempt to develop practices operating in secular school: aggressive competition, the premium placed upon worldly success, the use of selfish rewards ... the need for outward conformity in social attitudes.

As an ecclesial community the Catholic school must also develop its central mission which is to develop the faith identity of its members principally through communal worship. As James Arthur (1995:57) noted:

The individual Christian's need for belonging and social interaction, for clarification and interpretation of their life's experiences and for their responsible participation in adult roles should be met by the local Church – the community of believers. This happens essentially through scripture, creeds, liturgy, and the sacraments, but also through Catholic schooling, which together represent a concrete religion–philosophical system wholly absent in secular schools.

Certainly, State schools are marked by a greater plurality of teachers, students, beliefs, attitudes and so on. It is not social justice that is Catholicism's main focus, but salvation, since Catholic education cannot limit itself to the claim that there are objective social goods. As John Haldane, (1996:135) says: 'the primary function of Catholic schools is to transmit Catholic truths and Catholic values. Everything else, no matter how important, is secondary to this'. Therefore, a Catholic school cannot accept any communitarian thought that confines its aims and activities to producing good citizens who participate in democratic processes. Catholicism rejects the notion of religion and politics merging and completely rejects the idea of a national civic religion.

A Catholic communitarian view of education and the school curriculum would include the promotion of religious values which are genuinely held and shared and which bind teachers, pupils and parents together with a collective understanding of purpose. This notion of the school would be above expediency and pragmatics. Byrk et al. (1993:279) asserts that it is the underlying values of the Catholic school which are shared by its members that provide the 'animating force for the entire enterprise'. However, there needs to be a critical mass of Catholic pupils and staff who seek to motivate the rest of the school community, who must be open to such influence, in shaping the values of the school. Bradley's (1996) organizational structure of 'shepherd leadership' provides an interesting description of what a Christian school would look like within a communitarian framework and she lists seven characteristics:

1 a strong unity of purpose around a central vision;
2 a commitment to individual growth in the context of community;
3 a sense of belonging;
4 a recognition of functions differentiated according to gift;
5 the irrelevance of status;
6 a sense of shared responsibility;
7 interdependence of the members.

In this model the whole school community becomes one dynamic unit, inter-related, interconnected, and interdependent. The religious ethos of the school would be led by those who enunciate a moral character ideal. These high levels of commitment to values might explain the academic success of Catholic schools. The Church seeks to form a Christian community which will also participate and make a positive contribution to the building of a just and moral society. The aim of the school curriculum is to develop the individual skills and understanding to participate in society for the Catholic school must be of service to the wider community. The teacher is not limited to the transmission of knowledge but he or she is also an 'educator' helping to form the human person.

A Catholic communitarian education would also clearly embrace the idea that morality is learnt within the context of a religious tradition, Catholicism itself being this moral tradition with its own standards of excellence and world view. Catholic education would also encourage loyalty and responsibility to the communities that have nurtured them: the family, Church and school. It is why Catholic educators insist that we should develop the child's emotional attachment to these communities and their moral codes before cultivating the child's reason. The justification offered for this reasoning is that they believe that morality is not taught only rationally, but also by ceremony and rhetoric. Individuals are therefore educated into a tradition and moral behaviour is to speak of the specific practices of traditions or virtues associated with those traditions. However, a Catholic communitarian view could not sanction any and every community-grounded norm for morality, since it advocates transcendent norms and ideals for a moral education. Consequently, religious schools have the potential to adopt, if they have not already, a strong version of the communitarian ideal of education. While communitarians encourage the formation of diverse community-based organizations so as to enable citizens to work together in pursuit of common objectives, many of them find certain difficulties with Church groups which are not inclusive. With the great spectrum of religious life in society we can find particular examples of religious schools that range from being entirely open towards the outside community to nearly totally isolated. Some communitarians, together with liberals, fear that religious institutions can have an unsatisfactory side to them which may include parochialism, conformity, assimilation, and distrust of outsiders. It is why they are generally much less clear about how they should feel about the recent proliferation of voluntary groups centred on religious and ethnic identity. Mark Halstead (1995) adopts a communitarian perspective on religious schools when he argues liberalism threatens the cultural and religious identities of non-liberal minorities by exposing them to liberal culture of personal autonomy. He specifically refers to Muslim communities and argues for a balance between civic and cultural commitments in democratic societies. However, Neil Burtonwood (1998) seriously doubts whether this is possible since liberalism cannot be neutral between those cultures that value individual autonomy and those that do not.

Stanley Hauerwas (1981) is a prominent American Christian communitarian who believes that in a liberal society the very language of Christian education is in total opposition to the language of autonomy. He asserts that a religious communitarian perspective means that children would have to give up certain 'freedoms' in order to belong to a nurturing community or 'community of virtues'. For him, the teaching of virtue can only occur when a community has an agreed narrative that includes a transcendent purpose to its existence. This would involve obedience to a religious authority through acceptance of the values, traditions and revelations of that religious authority. Hauerwas believes that it is within the Christian narrative that a virtuous life can best be cultivated. Robert Nash (1997:57) calls this a 'sectarian communitarianism' and, while he offers a number of criticisms of Hauerwas's position, he details a number of important contributions that religious organizations can make to education and civic democracy. Nash concludes that: 'Democracy is desperately in need of many of the more conservative sectarian virtues: self-sacrifice, humility, charity, faith, hope, love, patience, even a sense of redemption' (1997:87). Another insight that 'sectarians' offer in Nash's view is that they recognize that schools are caught between two conflicting missions:

> Either the schools and colleges default on their obligation to teach Judeo-Christian virtues in favour of cultivating those academic and technical competencies calculated to get students into first-rate colleges, graduate schools, and careers – or they become social service agencies whose charge is to bolster students' self-esteem and liberate a number of minority groups from their 'oppression'. Rarely, in the view of the sectarians, do they hear schools and colleges express much interest in matters of religion, faith, character, or virtue – for them, issues that form the irreducible core of genuine community life.
>
> (Nash 1997:85)

However, Nash's real problem with the religious communitarian view is that it may offend non-believers in a secular society. He appears interested in a religious communitarian perspective so long as it supports and enhances social justice and equality.

The Family and Religion

It is with family values, as we saw in Chapter 2, that the moral tone of communitarian writing is often most evident and consequently many communitarians encounter most controversy, particularly from feminists, when they support the idea that responsibility in parenting should be equally shared between the father and mother. British communitarians are certainly not calling for the restoration of the traditional family nor are they proposing a repressive majoritarianism, although not a few critics have interpreted it thus. Christianity has been a formative influence on our notion of the family in Western culture. Today, Christianity continues to promote the idea of the family, even the egalitarian family unit with husband and wife both sharing equally in the responsibilities of family life. While the Catholic Church continues to be more conservative in sexual ethics and has a greater emphasis on the intact family, it also supports a liberal social philosophy that is supportive of social welfare provided by the State. With many communitarians, Catholics believe that there is a crisis in the modern family caused by increased individualism and poor socialisation of children within family life.

However, the Catholic Church teaches that the family is also the first home of the Church; it is where parents introduce their children to the community of faith and the spiritual life. The family is an essential community of nurture to support human flourishing. The Church teaches that parents have rights and responsibilities, that the State must respect these rights by assisting them, but that this assistance must be limited to enabling parents to exercise their responsibilities. In other words, the State must not interfere in these parental prerogatives to bring their children up according to their own beliefs. This is why the Catholic family cannot allow the State school to become isolated from the influences of the family and it is why the Catholic Church advocates that schools should be closer to families, something many communitarians also advocate. The Catholic Church also seeks its own schools in certain cultures, usually in Anglo-Saxon Protestant cultures, where the influence of the Catholic family is often totally excluded from State education. For Catholics, the school is always supplementary to the family. A number of communitarians, as we have seen, believe that a central aim of education is social cohesion which is often turned into a religious hope. Communitarians who have this hope are generally antagonistic to Catholic schools for they see a particular community withdrawing its children from the socializing process in totally State-run education.

In Catholic teaching, the educational formation of a person cannot be understood without first considering the role of the family in this process. The family forms the first and most persistent influence on the character of young people and is prior to the individual. Thus, the Catholic Church states in the *Charter of the Rights of the Family* (1985: Art. 5): 'Since they have conferred life on their children, parents have the original, primary and inalienable right to educate them; hence they must be acknowledged as the first and foremost educators of their children'. Parents also have the right to select the best means, according to their religious and moral convictions, to educate their children. Therefore, educational pluralism, not State monopoly over education, is needed to guarantee these parental rights. In *Familiaris Consortio* (1981: Art. 44), *The Role of the Christian Family in the Modern World*, Pope John Paul II says: 'The social role of families is called upon to find expression also in the form of political intervention; families should be the first to take steps to see that the laws and institution of the State not only do not offend but support and positively defend the rights and duties of the family'. The principle of subsidiarity, which many communitarians endorse, is important in this context. It means that the responsibility to meet basic human needs rests first with the competent individuals, and only then with the group. Higher levels of community assume the responsibility only when the more basic unit either cannot or will not assume it. When applied to education the primary right belongs to the family, since the State must respect the wishes of the parent. The State should only intervene when there is abuse or neglect of children, for the child is not a creature of the State. The Church recognizes the modern fragmentation of the family through the high divorce rate and the fact that an increasing proportion of children are born outside of marriage and raised by single parents, but this does not change the rights of parents. Nor does it change the teaching of the Catholic Church on these matters even when it recognizes what some have called the 'culture of non-marriage'. Nevertheless, on a pastoral basis the Catholic Church can no longer make the traditional assumptions about the typical family in its membership.

There are a number of competing views of the three basic agencies in education, the State, family and individual, in contemporary British education. There are also tensions within contemporary thought as to who is the principal agent. First, there is a view of the State in which one particular conception of the good life is true and must be widely shared if human life is to be fulfilled. The State thus becomes the exclusive authority over education and promotes its view. This is seen in the National Curriculum and in the control and training of teachers. It is the State that determines what is to be taught and increasingly how it is to be taught. Teachers in this view become less like 'educators' and more like civil servants required to deliver a predetermined curriculum. Second, there is a view of the family which believes that parents are more likely to protect their own children's interest, or that parents have a natural right to shape the education of their children. Parents in these views determine what is to be taught – not the government. This can be seen in some Church schools, but particularly in private schools and philosophically based schools which are not subject to the National Curriculum. In defending the rights of parents, the Church is often accused of defending its own perceived rights. In its defence the Church would argue that while parental rights are fundamental in the choice of school, these rights must be balanced against those of the whole Catholic community. Therefore, Catholic schools are not to function in isolation from each other or from the Catholic community in general. Third, in the individualist view there are conceptions of education that assert that education should not favour any one vision of the good, but schools should simply provide each individual with enough information to make up his or her own mind. The proper authorities are therefore the professionals who are neutral toward competing values and ideals. We have seen this in many modern philosophies of education and some professional organizations in education still seek to achieve this aim.

The reality is that there is a combination of all of these views operating in our present system, but with a distinct move in the direction of the State model. Many people who hold a strong religious faith feel that this is a dangerous tendency as it does not incorporate fully the role of parents in the education of children, especially when they see their 'choice' of school limited to the options made available by the government. However, we need also to recognize that the perception that some parents have of their obligations as parents is very weak. This allows the State to increase its authority over education. There are in fact two main reasons why the State should be involved in education. First, while education is an individual good (individuals benefit from education), it is also a public good (society benefits from educated people). Second, not all parents will make the right choice for their children, and justice demands that the agents of the State make certain that the education provided for them is appropriate. There is obviously an ethical obligation on us all to care for all the children in our midst, especially those children whose parents are unable or unwilling to make effective choices of school.

Nevertheless, there appears to be a paradox of increasing State control in order to free individuals from the power of the State and the paradox of greater homogenization in the name of protecting diversity. It is why the most dangerous theories for religious people are those that see in the State, however defined, the ultimate end to which all else should be directed. The State in England and Wales determines the school curriculum, controls, owns and organizes the schools and even to some extent has the power to direct pupils to certain schools. In terms of morality, the State has long realized that it cannot restore unity to the common life of the community on the basis of Christian beliefs and values. Therefore it is forced to create an alternative, a 'myth' or 'civic religion', to be at the centre of national unity. Conflict between religion and the State is inevitable since an explicit religious faith embedded within a community would certainly represent an obstacle to the spread of civic religion. Fred Clarke (1938:2) recognized in the 1930s that this development of the all powerful State would be 'committed to a particular philosophy of life and seeking to organise the whole of life in accordance with a particular doctrine of the end of man's existence, and in an all-embracing community life which claims to be at once the source and the goal of all human activity: a State, that is to say, which aims at being also a Church'. Some versions of communitarianism have a clear tendency in this direction.

Conclusion

Catholic social thought differs fundamentally from liberalism and many versions of communitarianism and, while it has no difficulty in accommodating community as such, Catholics need to be clear about which community is under discussion. First, Catholicism advocates limited government as the State exists to serve the person in society. Catholic teaching believes that there is a limit to political authority, while many communitarians do not accept this limitation, since they are more interested in establishing the Kingdom of the World. Communitarians often see the State as the sole source of authority and the only legitimate representative of society. Bellah for example is really engaged in the divinization of politics for within his scheme of things man takes the place of God. Catholics believe that the individual does not live for the State since the State provides no reason for being. Second, it makes the distinction between Church and State with the Church free to discharge its mission. The Catholic Church sees itself as a counterbalance to the State and therefore it must be visible and active in the social order, but also independent of the political order. Catholicism has its own distinctive intellectual tradition, as Mary Keys (1996:10–11) says: 'human beings are neither the polis animals of classical antiquity nor the autonomous selves of contemporary liberal theory'. Catholic teaching can provide a theory of the importance of the individual who is the focal point of life and at the same time insists on the social nature of the individual and the primacy of the common good. The Church also recognizes the importance of civic virtue, participation and the public spirit. Many Catholics may agree with many of the rhetorical comments of communitarians, but for very different reasons, and they may well seek very different consequences. Since many Catholics also confuse the language of communitarianism with the language of Christian discipleship their Christianity appears more and more to stand not for transcendence, but for polity and ideology. Public philosophy communitarianism can appear to be hopelessly utopian in attempting to 'restore' the perfect community, where we substitute the ideal of community for the reality of individualism. Communitarians attempt to shift our focus from the individual as the centre of action and choice to the community as some sort of greater entity, but this is incompatible with the Catholic notion of the need for individual grace and redemption.

Joseph Budziszewski (1995) makes it clear that any programme of public philosophy that makes the temporal community the starting point for ethical or political theory is at odds with Christianity. He describes three types of communitarianisms, each of which is incompatible with Christianity:

> The demonic variety makes the community itself the source of value; the accountable variety submits the community to values of which it is not the source, but which can be identified by all; and the narrative variety submits it to values of which it is not the source, but which cannot be identified by all.

He identifies the first variety with the discredited ideology of *The People*, which was epitomized by Nazi Germany. In this chapter we have described a weaker form of this version of communitarian nationalism that sees a widely shared American culture as a requirement of democracy and of social stability. In this variety of communitarianism the individual enters into union with the people through his devotion to the State and through merging his own individuality into one great association. Budziszewski identifies the second variety with the public philosophy communitarians led by Etzioni, while the third variety he associates with communitarian theorists such as McIntyre. The second group stress the importance of communal integrity, but firmly deny that the community is the criterion of truth or that values are good because they originate in a community. They believe that community values should be judged by external and overriding criteria which are based on shared human experience. However, public philosophy communitarians, while stressing that all schools should teach morality, are effectively unable to answer the question: Whose morals are you to teach? The answer that we should teach the values that American or British people share is inadequate for it leads to compromise and generalities with no specific commitments, for example, many public philosophy communitarians believe in the dignity of all persons, but are in no way offended by abortion. The third variety believe that the story which a community tells is the only way that community has of understanding itself. As Budziszewski (1995) says the lesson is stark and immutable: 'That which makes sense of shared experience is not itself a shared experience; that which makes common humanity intelligible is not itself common to all humanity'. These are really particularistic communities since their values and traditions are not and need not be shared with everyone in the larger society. He concludes by warning Christians that:

> secular humanists have their own 'communitarianism' – a counter-accommodation, involving different groups, with different stories, sharing a different common ground – and these two communitarianisms are utterly at odds. In order to know which ground one can occupy, one must decide whose story is true. There is no other way.

Catholic schools, like Muslim, Hindu and Jewish schools, are particularistic institutions in which children share and live a story. These schools teach and pursue shared values and commitments and their religious moral tradition is constitutive of their community. The religious school as a community forms human connections and socializes the young into moral traditions and valued practices that can often appear non-liberal. The communal ethos within these religious schools often enhances their organizational effectiveness and in turn improves student academic performance. This communal ethos is often elusive, but it consists of a real weaving of traditions, beliefs, rituals and stories into the way people speak and act. The Catholic Church and other religious faiths, represented by their particular community of faith, believe that they have the right to found schools in a democracy that are in accordance with their conception of life that is in force in family and community. They reject the idea that liberal society can construct a rationally binding morality on all human beings or that cultural difference is an inessential and transitory incident in human life. Public philosophy communitarians appear to share the liberal belief that cultural identities are simply chosen lifestyles whose proper place is in private life divorced from the public realm. Religious traditions believe that cultural identities are not acts of choice, but arise through inheritance and community formation. All the major religions are deeply character-building and nurture the virtues of love, mercy, truth, care towards others and compassion. Therefore, in a pluralistic society, there should be an acceptance of a diversity of traditions and of conflicting cultural and religious forms. These religious forms or groups work within a society which is liberal and individualist rather than collectivist. John Gray (1994) argues that both liberalism and communitarianism ignore the differences among communities:

In the world of human history, as distinct from that of communitarian theory, communities make rival claims on territories they inhabit together, they are animated by conflicting narratives and cultural traditions, they renew their identities across the generations by strategies of exclusion and subordination, and so on. The real agenda for political thought – ignored by the new liberals and by their communitarian critics – is given by the conflicting claims of communities ... It is this agenda of relations among communities having irresolvably conflicting, and sometimes incommensurable claims, that the new liberalism, together with the standard criticisms of it, steadfastly ignores.

Gray proposes that we should devise a *modus vivendi* to facilitate harmonious co-existence among different communities through balancing the claims and interests in a political settlement. The Dual System of religious and secular schools in Britain is such an example of a political settlement – America has denied such a settlement to its citizens in favour of a civil religion, or hegemonic ideology.

6 School Case Studies: Communitarian Practices?

> The learning community is the foundation for all our futures. On the one hand, it makes the medium the message. In a world where the discovery of a sense of community within and especially across groups, associations and nations is so crucial an issue, learning about community through living it, and not just studying it, is the only way to prepare ourselves for the immense challenges ahead. On the other hand, the learning community is essential if education itself is to come alive and enable people to reach their full potential. Deprive learners of this communal context and education becomes a turgid and sluggish affair. Only as schools become more fully learning communities can education be transformed, as well as itself become a means of transformation.
>
> (D. Clark 1996:81)

The previous chapters have examined some of the historical and theoretical background to the communitarian agenda in education, and described how it is often associated with certain central concepts and terms. These concepts, such as responsibility, community, duty, respect and citizenship, can have an emotional appeal, but will remain quite meaningless without a firm understanding about what they mean in practice and how they might be developed in schools. In other words, whatever virtues there may be in communitarian approaches, it is vital that we are able to see how they might express themselves in actual classrooms, schools and communities. A difficulty with this goal, however, is that much of the literature in recent years on communitarian education originates in the United States and is founded upon the assumptions of the American system (O'Neill 1994). How is this relevant to the United Kingdom? After all, one of the presumptions of the communitarian approaches is that communities have distinctive characters, values and history; these are facts that no educational policy or practice can afford to ignore.

This chapter includes of a number of studies of English schools. None explicitly claim an affiliation with the communitarian agenda, indeed when visited most seemed unaware that such an agenda existed. However, each school has implemented a series of practices that are firmly grounded in a community-based approach to education. The suggestion here is that whatever terms the adults and children in these schools might use, they often share some of the assumptions regarding the merit of placing community at the heart of pupils' school experience. This chapter begins with brief examinations of each of the schools, and describes the community-based activities. It attempts to identify key themes that have emerged from the studies. It is important to acknowledge that the studies that make up this chapter form a very small sample. There is no attempt to offer a generalized picture of English schools. On the contrary, each of the schools has been selected precisely because it exhibits, in specific aspects, good and effective practice. No attempt was made to select schools with a specific understanding of the community dimension; as will become clear, unanimity is far from being achieved in this respect. A number of state schools were visited, and from these, three are examined below: a technology college, a secondary school and a primary school. In each school senior staff, teachers, ancillary staff and pupils were interviewed. Policy documentation, inspection reports and, in one case, a published book were consulted to gain an understanding about the philosophies and practices underpinning each school's work. An attempt has been made to visit schools from divergent geographical and social backgrounds.

Highfield Junior School, Plymouth

Highfield School is located in a large post-war housing estate on the outskirts of Plymouth. The majority of the children come from that estate, although some come from recently developed private housing. The incidences of unemployment and single-parent families in the area are high, and the school has a relatively high proportion of children receiving free school meals. A number of pupils enter school with language difficulties or with emotional and behavioural problems, and almost half the pupils in the school have been identified as having learning or related problems. Parents and school staff express concerns regarding the social and physical environment in which the pupils grow up: buildings in the estate (including the school) are frequently vandalized and there is evidence of drugs use by local people in the school grounds (in the form of syringes found on the playground).

For some years parents and teachers have worked to address the particular needs of children attending the school, but a significant point in the school's recent development was the appointment in 1995 of a new head teacher. She has recently moved on, but set in motion a wide-ranging series of innovations and changes that were very influential. Described variously as 'visionary', 'incredibly charismatic' and 'very supportive', the head teacher facilitated what some teachers describe as a 'revolution' within the school. Behaviour was identified as a particular concern, with reports of ill-discipline, disrespectful attitudes towards adults and a lack of motivation cited by staff working at the time. Of course, it is difficult in hindsight to assess the extent of the changes, but an OFSTED (Office for Standards in Education) report written less than a year after the appointment of the new head teacher applauds the behaviour of the pupils as 'good, having a positive effect on the standards of achievement, the quality and range of learning and the overall quality of life in the school' (OFSTED: 22 January 1996). That report also describes the pupils' social and moral development as exceptionally good, and identifies the leadership and commitment of the Head Teacher as a particular strength of the school. There is a sense of pride in the changes brought about in the school over the last few years. Indeed, the school has produced a book (Highfield Junior School 1997) that describes some of the changes and some of the activities carried out in the school.

The explicit foci of the changes brought about since 1995 are behaviour management and citizenship, but underlying both of these is an implicit aim to foster within the pupils, teachers, parents and other adults associated with the school a sense of community, and from this feelings of belonging and responsibility. Without seeking to undermine the contribution of any individual, the changes brought about were the result of a whole school approach to planning and implementation. An important medium for the school's development was the fostering of a sense of shared involvement and value. While acknowledging the need for leadership and direction, those working and attending the school also stressed the need for participation at every level of the school, from the head teacher and teachers, through classroom assistants and other adult support staff to pupils of every age.

The inspection report notwithstanding, this seems to be the truly distinctive feature of the school: it has created and works to maintain a community in which every member feels that he or she has a role to play and can have his or her voice heard. As the school's book states:

> Some schools try to change by using only the teachers' ideas. But that misses out on most of the energy and ideas in the school. It can lead to teachers trying to force their plans on the pupils, and the pupils trying to stop them. Instead, we looked at ways for the staff and pupils and parents to work together.
>
> (Highfield Junior School 1997:7)

This emphasis upon whole school participation is not an easy option, since the greater the rights and influence of the school community, the greater the responsibility to contribute. Some recognize that some of the proposed changes were slow to be accepted by all, but also point out that once they saw the changes to behaviour and learning, reception was more favourable. One classroom assistant who had witnessed the school's change of approach stated that previously she had never felt herself to be a member of staff, rather merely a visitor. The increased responsibility taken by all members of the school has resulted in a greater sense of investment in school affairs: 'I don't think I'd get the same satisfaction at another school as I do here. We are heavily involved in all aspects of the school.' Likewise, a group of 10-years-olds discussing the school's policy agreed that they felt under some pressure to set examples to younger children and to take on the extra responsibilities of the school community, but also conceded that 'it's easy if you get used to it' and that 'this is the way everybody wanted it to be' (Year 6 pupils).

An important step in changing the school, and in developing a more fulfilling and secure community within it was to establish a clear and agreed code of discipline. It is felt that for many children school is the one place that can be relied upon to be safe, secure and consistent, and this is the kind of environment the school staff seek to provide for them: 'The first thing we had to do was to gain control, to create boundaries within which we could teach and the children could learn. So we started using assertive discipline' (Highfield Junior School 1997:8). Assertive discipline is reasonably well established in British primary schools, and while its implementation varies from institution to institution, its focus is generally upon a clear and explicit structure of behaviour management and punishment. Pupils who break school rules are given a series of warnings and punishments of increasing seriousness. The emphasis is upon each child's individual responsibility to behave in an appropriate manner, and since the rules and consequences of breaking them are explicit and frequently discussed, the child is seen as choosing a particular course of action.

The school places great importance upon Circle Time, which is a technique designed to encourage open communication and the sharing of ideas. Initially used as an opportunity to teach the children to listen and discuss feelings, it has developed into a central mechanism for facilitating the school's wider aims. The basic rules of a class Circle Time are simple:

* only talk one at a time;
* be kind to others and don't say anything that will be hurtful;
* listen carefully;
* talk clearly so that everyone can hear you.

Teachers have noticed improvements in spoken language, and the opportunity for children to discuss their concerns and feelings in a non-threatening setting has encouraged greater understanding of others and a more developed sense of belonging; as a classroom assistant stated: 'I think if they're happy at school and can share their feelings with their class friends, they won't feel worried and lonely. That's not going to play on their minds, and they're going to concentrate on their work more' (Highfield Junior School 1997:11).

Underlying the school's approach to discipline is an assumption that if children are to act as members of the school's community, they need to take a degree of responsibility for their actions. The deputy head teacher discussed this in terms of making all the pupils aware of their choices, freedoms and responsibilities: 'the school community can only be developed through informing children of the choices available to them in life'. Circle Time has also been used as a tool for enforcing this message by creating a forum for making decisions. So, children discuss and decide school rules and conventions, and also help deal with problems like bullying. In the words of a senior teacher, the school is 'the children's society, a web of networks. It is not merely like society, but their actual society'. The assumption made by the members of the school is that decisions and negotiations at the group level of the class offer a greater authority to certain policies and rules.

The philosophy that all members of the school have both rights and duties to participate in certain decisions was developed through the establishment of the School's Council, which is made up of representatives of each class (except the very youngest). Meeting every fortnight, the Council acts as of an extension of Circle Time, exploring whole school issues, as well as sharing the concerns, needs, ideas and successes of each class. Minutes are taken so that representatives can report back to their classes in Circle Time. Topics might include extra-curricular clubs, playground behaviour and the use of the Council's small budget. An associated whole school issue in which the pupils participate is the selection of new teachers. While the final decision is always left with the school's governing body, children from each class meet with all candidates for posts, including senior posts. Rather than placing children in judgment of adults, the procedure is intended to identify the qualities and skills each person can bring to the school. As the head teacher at the time put it:

> We always take account of the children's views. We listen simply to what they think each applicant can contribute to school life. We decide first and then we read out the children's decision. The children's and the adults' interview panel have always chosen the same person.
>
> (Highfield Junior School 1997:40)

A number of the school's policies derive from a philosophy of education for democracy. Preparation for an active role in society is a theme underpinning a great deal of the schemes discussed. In fact, the general Curriculum Statement begins with the following claim:

> Our pupils will soon have the opportunity to take their place as voting citizens in a democratic society. It is very important that the education they receive during these formative years should prepare them for the rights, responsibilities, duties and obligations which accompany the role of citizens in our rapidly changing world.

In recent years, a number of projects have been added to the curriculum that address more directly the stated need for education for active citizenship. A Citizenship Award has just been introduced for the oldest pupils (10 and 11-year-olds), whereby they must show that they have successfully completed a series of tasks associated with being an active member of the school community and contributing to the wider community. Winners of the award must regularly attend one of the numerous extra-curricular sports and activities available, participate in First Aid Training, undertake a residential visit and ensure excellent school attendance. Pupils must also take part in some form of community service or, as it is increasingly coming to be known, Service Learning. The age of the pupils means that the range of learning opportunities is necessarily limited, but activities include visiting old age pensioners at their homes, assisting in the local library and helping younger children through a paired reading scheme.

In January 1998 the Junior School amalgamated with the neighbouring Infant School and the former's head teacher took the opportunity to move on to other work. Therefore, a new school was created, with new leadership and a number of new members of staff. The new head teacher was supportive of the school's policies on behaviour, community and citizenship, as was the senior management. However, a number of teachers identified a change to the social dynamic within the school, and there has been concern that the changes brought about in the Junior School would come to an end; as one teacher put it, since the amalgamation, 'the changes have gone from a raging boil to luke-warm'. Time will tell whether the school will be able to regain the momentum and direction that has characterized its recent history.

Battersea Technology College, London

Battersea Technology College is a relatively small school, situated in central London. Its intake is mixed, but a large number of pupils come from impoverished backgrounds: the proportion of pupils qualifying for free school meals is significantly above the average for similar institutions. A high proportion of pupils have an identified Special Educational Need, including difficulties in the use of language and emotional and behavioural problems. Attainment in General Certificate of Secondary Education (GCSE) in most subjects, including the core subjects of English, mathematics and science, are below the national average. However, the rate of improvement in these results has steadily increased during recent years.

Changes to the school's fortunes seem to coincide with changes to the management and organization of the College. After an unsuccessful OFSTED inspection, re-organization and a series of amalgamations, a large number of new appointments were made, including a restructured management team and a new principal in 1996. The new administration found itself faced with a host of problems, including falling academic standards, truancy and bullying. Staff morale was low, there were many temporary staff, and the opportunities for such extra-curricular activities as sport, drama and music were very limited. Fundamental to each of these, however, was a lack of identity, and the first step in the process of changing the college was developing a strong sense of community.

At the heart of the college's conception of community was the concept of shared values, without which objectives such as educational performance and appropriate behaviour would be impossible. The new principal describes the aim as follows:

> You cannot talk about education without talking about citizenship and community ... You are moulding the students into something you might call a community, but essentially you are talking about values. What are you trying to create homogeneously across the community?

The lack of a coherent sense of identity and community is cited by staff and older pupils as an important factor in past difficulties, and many blame a lack of direction and communication for growing disorder and violence.

Rather than simply enforcing a set of values and standards upon the college, the principal and senior staff instigated numerous meetings, both formal and informal, involving members of staff, students and the wider community. The majority of staff and students were keen for change, so discussion took place to find common ground. It was felt self-evident that existing attitudes that had evolved in some parts of the college, such as 'anything goes', 'the strongest is the best' and 'don't care for anyone or anything apart from oneself', were damaging to all. Therefore, before any specific innovations were introduced, a period of stabilization took place, in which all those involved in the college's work contributed to the articulation of shared values. The values that were discussed were not extraordinary or original; on the contrary, they reflect the core values of a community discussed earlier in the book: self-worth, respect for others, trust, sharing and responsibility. Also, as one member of staff put it, they constitute the basic principles of any successful school:

> The principles on which all learning takes place; the principles on which good order is established; the principles on which growing into adulthood occurs; and it is a question of finding out how that common understanding is shaped up with your institution against this particular set of beliefs that makes it work.

Once the core values were established within the school, a range of initiatives were introduced to develop their expression in more concrete forms. Older pupils now undertake placements in local nursery schools, businesses and local environment improvement schemes. They also have the opportunity to take part in voluntary activities, through liaison with outside agencies like the Community Service Volunteers. At the same time, a structured scheme, an extended enrichment studies programme, offers different age groups different foci, each related to community and citizenship. During their first four years at the college, pupils undertake modules that consider improvement of the school environment, work in the local community, developing the school community, and working with local businesses. Each module offers the students the opportunity to contribute to the school's development in specific and tangible ways, while reinforcing core values. For example, students focusing upon developing the school community at the time of writing are researching the type and extent of bullying, with the intention of informing new policy.

An implicit theme within much of the work is the idea of the college as a community in itself. Through articulating the shared values of its members, agreeing standards of behaviour and encouraging active participation in some decision-making, the intention is that students will take a degree of responsibility for the college and their peers. From this foundation, it is hoped that they will have a sense of worth in their school and in themselves. A number of teachers described a widespread lack of self-esteem among the children in previous years. More recently, however, they have started to detect a change; in the words of one teacher:

> Somewhere along the line, throughout all the school now ... the pupils all think, 'We are worth something' ... The ethos has really changed ... The one thing that has really changed is a sense of value in themselves.

This theme, the college as a community, relates to another stated aim: the college as a safe place for the pupils. The local area in which the college is situated contains a number of harmful elements such as violence, drug abuse and vandalism, from which the pupils ought to be protected. This is recognized by the principal:

> Whilst you might say that a school is a microcosm of the society out there, I do hope that Battersea College isn't actually a microcosm of the society the students live in. It is a safe place; it is a

place where the values in relation to one's own well-being and the welfare of others is being promoted all the time.

Thus, the college aims to be a protective community; that is, one in which pupils feel safe from threats that may exist outside it. At the same time, it is a community in which you try to develop values which maybe, 'when they grow up, they will take on as being better than the one's they experience elsewhere' (principal).

There would seem to be some tension between the aims of initiating pupils into and protecting them from the wider community, and it is not immediately obvious how it can be resolved. Of course, this is not a problem for Battersea College alone; it faces many State schools. Indeed, perhaps it is an inherent consequence of any community-based education approach.

Colne Community College, Essex

Colne College is a large secondary school, with a wide geographical catchment area. Attendance is good, parental unemployment is low and the proportion of students with Special Educational Needs is lower than the national average. The school's reputation in the local area is good, and it receives relatively strong support from parents and local businesses. Like the other schools studied, Colne College has under-gone re-organization of the senior management team during the last decade. Previously a high school 'with poor academic performance', the deliberate change of title to 'Community College' has coincided with a significant improvement of standards. Recent years have seen a period of consolidation and development, most noticeably in relation to the community dimension of the school's work.

The community-based innovations in the college are the most far-reaching and central of the schools visited. They are radical in the literal sense of the term: they go to the very centre of its day-to-day affairs and organization. The assistant principal claims that community forms a 'central focus' of changes, affecting management, curriculum and expectations. She likens the community focus to dropping a pebble in a pond; starting with the individual child at the centre, the ripples of rights and responsibilities spread to the form group, the school, the local environment, Europe and beyond. The rationale of this model is based upon a consensual dissatisfaction with the damaging effects of selfishness and individualism: 'It is about creating an atmosphere in which we try to challenge the ethos of the 1980s, of individualism'.

The values of the school, printed in all development plans, focus upon the quality of relationships between staff and students. They include consideration for others, honesty in one's dealings, working for the benefit of others and respect for individuals' rights, views and property. A recent OFSTED report (OFSTED: 14 September 1998) commended the college's pastoral system, in which the pastoral role of the form tutor is supplemented by a range of peer-led schemes, such as student mentors for victims of bullying and for pupils experiencing difficulties with academic work.

In emphasizing the view of the school as a community, it is felt vital by the leadership that all members of the college feel a sense of responsibility to the others and to the institution as a whole: 'We want students to feel that they have a part to play in the running of the school, and in the way that the school works', is the way the assistant principal expressed this approach. Thus, each form group elects a male and female representative to its Year Council, and each year group elects representatives for the School Council. Although this is a common feature of many secondary schools in the UK, the Colne Council has a particularly high profile and makes up a central component of the management and consultation processes. Some students are elected to the Student and Curriculum Standing Committee; others are part of specific action groups. In all cases, the intention is for pupils to take on a more active involvement in effecting change within the school community. Information resulting from these groups is then cascaded back to form groups. This approach has enabled students at Colne College to have a particularly well-developed understanding of events and developments within the school.

Older students are encouraged to take on additional responsibilities. A number are recommended by their peer members to act as senior student representatives'. Some senior pupils are trained as peer-led teachers in a range of subject areas, including literacy, numeracy, drugs education, and an innovative and a highly regarded sex education scheme. Other students represent the college at meetings of the local regeneration group, at local literary societies, local business and industry organizations, environmental groups and even at the Town Council.

Like the other schools studied, community-based work has been extended through the involvement of outside agencies. 'Changemakers' is a student-led project in which pupils take part in neighbourhood schemes; the common theme to each scheme, as described by one student, is 'to make a difference in our community'. Students are encouraged to visit different sites within the neighbourhood, interview local people and devise their own projects, such as fund-raising and charity events, organized with support from staff and community groups. Specific sessions are time-tabled for the youngest year group, in which they are guided and supported in organizing community-based activities. From this foundation, successive year groups are required to give their own time to the work, after school.

Each of the schools studied benefited from contact with the Community Service Volunteers (Education) organization, whose remit is to initiate and support community or Service Learning developments in schools. In the case of the Colne College, it was felt that any developments of this sort needed to be 'fully embedded in the curriculum', in the words of a senior teacher, rather than merely an add-on or associated with a small group of interested staff. Therefore, each subject faculty is required to plan Service Learning opportunities so that by the end of their schooling, all pupils will have experienced a structured and meaningful community-based activity in each aspect of the curriculum. Guided and evaluated by an appointed Community Liaison Officer, these activities have recently included the following: Advanced Level students in Expressive Arts produced a video on school life for each of the primary schools in the area; 13 and 14-year-olds interviewed older members of the local community in order to develop a working historical archive; Child Development courses involve regular placements in playgroups, nursery and primary schools; in their Technology lessons, 11 and 12-year-olds designed and built equipment for the Town's Horticultural society; pupils studying Geography researched and took part in environmental protection work. In all cases, the emphasis is upon engaging students in meaningful participation alongside interested groups and individuals within the community and on making the school itself a resource of that community.

The model of school leadership is, in the words of the principal, 'principle-centred', whereby the values of the school underpin and direct practice. As has been seen, these values emphasize the place of each member of the college within a series of communities: the form group, the school, the local area, and so on. The outcome of this approach seems to be a strong sense of responsibility among the students and staff to the different levels of community, as well as an understanding of the processes involved. One teacher who has recently arrived at the school identifies this aspect of its work as particularly distinctive, and uses words reminiscent of much communitarian writing on the subject: 'Students gain self-confidence and self-awareness, an increased sense of responsibility, a wider understanding of being a citizen, and satisfaction from making a difference ... as well as knowledge of how difficult making a change can be'.

Selected Themes

The development of Community Education in the United Kingdom has been usefully chronicled by Clark (1996). Moving through a series of phases, from a small number of rural village colleges to more wide-scale urban developments, the Community Education Project has been characterized by an attempt to break down the barriers between schools and their wider community.

Some commentators have noted that much policy explicitly labelled 'community education' in the UK has been somewhat limited in its scope: an add-on to the main curriculum and function of the school; making school buildings available to the neighbourhood during evenings for adult courses and social events; employing a pre-school worker or a home–school link officer (Atkinson 1994:20). This approach is expressed in the influential report on Educational Priority Areas, where Halsey (1972:134) defined the community school as 'a school which is open beyond the ordinary school hours for the use of children, their parents and, exceptionally, for other members of the community' (although it needs to be acknowledged that this definition does not fully reflect the overall ethos of that report).

Clearly, the aspects of school that interface with the community have a valuable role to play, but each of the case studies of schools presented in this chapter have developed the concept much further, placing community at the very heart of their work as an aim, if not a practice. They, like a number of other schools, have envisaged an approach far more akin to that of the communitarians, in which the community dimension lies at the heart of school. A strong statement of this view is made by Cambridgeshire County Council (CCC), which was the home of the very earliest projects:

> Community education is not a department or a subdivision or a subject within the education service. It is a philosophy and a spirit which imbues all else. It is not the special job of a few, not an extra task on an educator's already overcrowded job description. It is the task of education itself.
>
> (CCC 1990:5)

129

A more systematic portrait of the range of understandings of community schooling is presented by Hargreaves (1982). He identifies four distinct approaches, although these would hardly seem to be exhaustive. Interestingly, each understanding was evident in the practices of each of the schools studied. One category is concerned with the development of a sense of community within the school; pupils experience a microcosm of democratic living through devolution of decision-making in certain prescribed areas. In the studies there was an implicit acceptance of the communal nature of the school, and even of the component classes within it; as Handy and Aitken (1986:14) put it, 'each class is but a mini-society within the larger society of the school'. The existence of a School's Council was common to the schools, and in each case the student representatives had a degree of involvement in school management; in one, pupils took part in the interview procedure for new members of staff; in another, the elected School's Council had a discretionary budget for improvements to the school environment; in the third, students worked alongside staff and governors on the curriculum group and other action groups. The schools also supported the widespread practice of elections to Year and School Councils. Of course, the extent of their participation was generally restricted to relatively marginal aspects of decision-making. However, most pupils felt involved in the running of the school and welcomed the opportunity to contribute in some way.

A second category relates to community participation in the school, through structures ranging from Parent–Teacher Associations and adult helpers in classrooms to community control over elements of the school. Parent groups and classroom support are universal in UK primary schools, as is community participation in the administration of the school affairs through the diverse membership of governing bodies. The primary school studied was particularly eager to integrate all adults who worked in the school on an equal standing, and this included an explicit policy in which distinctions between teaching staff and other adults were minimalized.

The third approach is concerned with the conception of the school as a community centre, in which members of the school and the neighbourhood share facilities, and the school acts as a natural centre for community meetings and activities:

> the school, like the doctors surgery or health centre, is the obvious meeting point for young parents ... It is possible to envisage the

... school as being not just a provider of education but also a centre for the whole family.

(Atkinson 1994:26)

Primary schools are particularly well-placed as natural gathering places for community groups as most parents visit every day, and they tend to be closer to home than the less numerous secondary schools. Secondary schools, on the other hand, boast far better specialist facilities and many more parents. All of the schools discussed offered a number of services to the community. The primary school, for example, invited pensioners to use their dining facilities for lunch and social gatherings. Both secondary schools offered classrooms and halls to different groups. The community college also housed the town's Sports Centre. Some schools, although none discussed in this chapter, have taken the extent of community control further, with the establishment of Community Councils. In these cases, the financial management (but not academic) of the school is shared by the school's management with representatives of the local community. In part, this development is a recognition of the enormous opportunity for use and income-generating potential of school resources, such as sports halls, Information Technology laboratories, music facilities, outside the relatively limited hours they are conventionally used. Whether schemes of this sort will work in all schools is uncertain, however, due to the resistance of many adults to returning to school. Both secondary schools studied commented upon the extreme difficulty they had found welcoming some sections of their local neighbourhood into their buildings.

The last understanding of community schooling is that of the community-centred curriculum, which might consist of pupils taking part in community service or in taking courses in community studies or citizenship. Understandably, the extent of the community service undertaken at the schools increased with the age of the pupils. The youngest children visited and supported voluntary groups in the neighbourhood, while the oldest experienced placements in local businesses, other schools and, in the case of one school, in areas of deprivation both in the UK and abroad. To some extent, then, all schools endorsed the inclusion of community-based activities within the curriculum. However, only the community college fully embraced the concept, with a large amount of the statutory requirements being met through a community-centred curriculum.

It is worthwhile mentioning an issue associated with the idea (or ideal?) of a community-centred schooling. A number of those interviewed cited the implementation of the Education Reform Act (1988) as a barrier to the implementation of community-based initiatives. One teacher (Highfield School) referred to the 'curriculum overload' resulting from the introduction of a compulsory and substantial National Curriculum. Another (Colne Community College) complained about the lack of flexibility in terms of planning and organization resulting from a prescriptive inspection policy. In fact, the changes brought about by the 1988 Education Reform Act led to trends that simultaneously strengthened and weakened the potential for community-based work in schools. Certainly, schools were led to much closer contacts with parents and local commerce than had previously been the norm. Moreover, the Act, in theory, seemed to support a role for community education, with its assertion that the National Curriculum should '[p]romote the spiritual, moral, cultural, mental and physical development of pupils at the school and of society; and prepare such pupils for the opportunities, responsibilities and experiences of adult life' (Education Reform Act 1988:1). Further documented support came in the Guidance Notes on Education for Citizenship, produced by the newly formed National Curriculum Council (1990:3):

> Pupils should develop knowledge and understanding of ... the nature of community: the variety of communities to which people simultaneously belong – family, school, local, national, European and world-wide; how communities combine stability and change; how communities are organised and the importance of rules and laws.

In practice, however, there exist clear threats to such approaches, including:

- an increasingly dominant focus on education as being about narrowly defined subjects and examinations;
- a form of local management of schools which would make the extra resources needed for community initiatives an expensive luxury;
- encouraged competition between schools, which might prevent sharing of experience, expertise and resources of value to the wider community.

(Clark 1996:17)

It is not certain how community education will develop in the schools discussed in this chapter, or, for that matter, any school in the

United Kingdom. The educational environment in which frequent changes of policy and guidance have left many teachers disorientated has led some to adopt a cautious stance to any curricular developments. Recent directives, for example on literacy and numeracy teaching in primary schools, may increase teachers' reluctance to extend the scope of their activity. Even if schools developed their work in this area, many might find themselves in need of much more specific guidance on its implementation than is currently available. Despite the imaginative work taking place within the schools discussed above, none was able to draw upon an established model of practice in the UK. As Hargreaves (1982:114) accurately states, 'The concept of the community school, like the concept of community itself, is a flabby and sometimes vacuous one'. As such, schools seem forced to adopt a policy of *ad hoc* improvisation, taking from diverse (and perhaps contradictory) sources to address an apparent need. If community is so fundamental to the development and well-being of children, as has been suggested, then this seems to be an unsatisfactory situation.

7 The Communitarian Agenda in Education

> The advocacy of communitarian reforms has a long history of achievement which supports our faith in their ability to secure a better community life for all in the years to come.
>
> (Henry Tam 1998:266)

Communitarianism achieves its most powerful expression in the thinking of academic theorists, such as Alasdair McIntyre, Michael Sandel and John Gray. We have seen how communitarian theorists believe that the community is a fundamental and irreplaceable part of the good life for human beings and that full participation in community life is important for experiencing this good life; further, the self is 'embedded' in and partly constituted by communal commitments and values that are not always objects of choice. Communitarianism has a focus on explaining how humans become what they are and it also has a normative dimension which says that community is a good thing. This complex type of thinking contrasts with the often rhetorical flow of much of the popular 'communitarian movement'. This 'communitarian movement', as represented by Etzioni, is less clear in its arguments, but nevertheless feels able to advocate substantial social policy measures at the centre of which is their strong call to refocus on community life and moral renewal. These measures often aim to function as a corrective to various forms of excessive individualism and seek to create a new order that certain communitarians would have us believe is without oppression or puritanism. Or is this 'communitarian movement' really just a sophisticated version of liberalism, tempering individualism with 'individualism within community'?

Most communitarians also implicitly accept the capitalist system and few propose more government intervention, but instead want to see more local effort and debate. David Anderson (1998:35) illustrates the point:

> To be avoided at all costs is the view that Etzioni's 'third way' is driven by the attempt to find innovative ways to motivate consumers and corporate leaders to do the right thing as they maximize their own well-being. While he does support certain kinds of policies that would provide economic incentives, he is much more interested in finding innovative ways to motivate people to help others from a standpoint of moral responsibility. His views on both economic and noneconomic behavior are clearly driven by his concerns for the moral voice.

Community is, therefore, a product of shared morals, not economic circumstances, which means that this version of communitarianism is hardly likely to be viewed by capitalists as a radical philosophy, since it fails to mount any serious challenge to the growing economic inequality in society. In the context of education Anthony Giddens (1998:109) reminds us that:

> Yet the idea that education can reduce inequality in a direct way should be regarded with some scepticism. A great deal of comparative research, in the US and Europe, demonstrates that education tends to reflect wider economic inequalities and these have to be tackled at source.

Communitarians also give emphasis to the idea of choice within communities, which means that those who are genuinely marginalized or feel powerless within a community could be viewed as responsible for their own shortcomings. The idea of 'dutiless rights' has been regularly popularized by the New Right rhetoric in order to move the agenda from rights to obligations. Communitarians appear to have no new answer for social inequality, for while many of them accept that all within society are deserving of the good life, their equality of opportunity does not provide this good life for all since unequal abilities and luck produce unequal social results. This can be the same as accepting human social inequalities and their consequences as natural. If New Labour is to take seriously their own slogans of 'one nation, one community' and the 'stakeholder society' then it needs to realize that it all depends upon a substantial redistribution of income wealth and life chances. John Gray (1994) also warns us that the communitarian literature tends to ignore the conflicting claims and relations among different communities within the overall nation. Derek Phillips (1993:176) goes further and says that there are many dangers with the pursuit of the communitarian ideal. Above all, we need to remember that there are perhaps as many communitarian positions as there are communitarian writers.

A summary of the core ideas in the communitarian agenda for education in schools which have been discussed in this book may be reduced to ten basic themes. All of them have policy implications for the way we educate young people. They are as follows.

1 The family should be the primary moral educator of children

The role of the family in education is at the core of the communitarian perspective. The focus lies with parenting rather than with marriage *per se*. The majority of communitarians align themselves with the two-parent model of the family as the most effective means to bring up children and they assert that there is an essential moral nature to the parenting role. Families headed by single parents, communitarians claim, experience particular difficulties. Both parents are therefore seen as responsible for ensuring that their children are socialized into the community and are educated to contribute to the community through their own participation in the community's life. A communitarian perspective generally places the primary duty on the moral education of children on both parents and, to varying degrees, on their extended family. Schools are seen, theoretically at least, as secondary moral educators, but since many children actually spend more time consistently in school than they do with their parents, schools are increasingly seen in the front line. However, even when there is 'parental deficit' parents are still to be encouraged to participate actively in their children's education through an active partnership with schools and teachers.

2 Character education includes the systematic teaching of virtues in schools

The majority of communitarians of all persuasions have been extremely critical of values clarification methods in schools and have instead advocated that schools should teach a common set of values or moral standards of behaviour as a way of dealing with social fragmentation. They do not offer any explicit set of moral values as they leave this to the community to devise. However, they do give greater emphasis to the concept of a virtue-centred education that is based on tradition. They generally reject ideas of values that can mean anything to any individual or group, at any time and for any reason, and they talk of avoiding children receiving a 'morally careless education' in schools. They argue that individual character and personality are therefore deliberately formed by teachers using a virtue-centred education – 'the second line of defence' argument. This raises the question of whether or not teachers and schools are prepared for such virtue-centred approach to the teaching of morality. Communitarians are divided about what virtues should be taught, especially between those virtues that benefit the individual and those that benefit the community. Overall, their whole conception is rather one of duty, and a duty expressed in terms of secular virtues.

3 The ethos of the community has an educative function in school life

A central theme in communitarian thinking is the stress placed on community as a human good, in particular, the importance of certain types of obligations and communal commitments and values that form the ethos of a school. A genuine community from a communitarian perspective is therefore one which is more than a mere association of individuals. It is, rather, a community that has common ends, not congruent private interests, but shared goals and values. Anything that furthers the mission of the school is considered a gain for each individual member of the school. Individuals in such a community are educated by the other members through their example, activities and full participation in the life of the community – the community models the good or just society. However, a strong ethos of the school may exert pressure on individuals to conform and even result in a lack of recognition of diversity within the school community. Indeed, children are generally of a school community which is not of their choosing.

4 Schools should promote the rights and responsibilities inherent within citizenship

Almost all communitarian thinking emphasizes the duties we owe to the community in return for the rights we enjoy as citizen members of that community. To claim certain rights within a community involves reciprocal duties which together integrate one into the community itself. Ideally, communitarians prefer that individuals feel responsible for others in the community for its own sake rather than out of feeling obliged to reciprocate. Nevertheless, communitarians are strongly supportive of citizen education programmes that aim to enhance social and moral responsibility in young people and above all educate them to be committed to full participation as citizens. There are two central issues in this thinking: first, citizenship is seen as something that is earned, not a right in itself; and second, the communitarian perspective on citizenship requires commitment and participation which is sometimes difficult for teachers to achieve within a school environment. The weakness in this thought concerns the fact that if teachers are to develop informed and effective citizens who are empowered with knowledge and skills in a changing society, then they require a clearer justification for their role in this than many communitarians offer at present. In addition, teachers are already engaged in citizenship education within their schools, the influence of which is often underestimated.

5 Community service is an important part of a child's education in school

Some prominent communitarians have campaigned for mandatory community service for all young people as a formal part of the school curriculum. The key to understanding this kind of communitarian thinking is to focus on the experiential learning that is being advocated. Schools are expected to provide young people with opportunities to work within their local community in order to build their characters and encourage them to form the habits to participate beyond school in community involvement projects. In addition, young people would be encouraged to work in teams and in so doing learn to form a community of service among themselves.

6 A major purpose of the school curriculum is to teach social and political life-skills

Communitarians would say that education should above all be directly concerned with the development of reflective thinking and social action through informed civic participation. The abilities for making socially productive decisions do not develop by themselves; rather, they require that the content of the school curriculum, skills and attitudes be introduced early and built upon throughout the years of schooling. The school curriculum should therefore promote those skills that are necessary for social and political literacy so that young people can make reasoned judgments, considering others' views and acting for the benefit of the community. Young people need to acquire civic skills which will include the ability to talk with each other, compromise with each other and engage in open exchange.

7 Schools should promote an active understanding of the common good

Another central theme in communitarian thinking concerns the idea of the 'common good'. Many communitarians believe that there exists a collective or public interest that can be promoted by individuals within communities. Education is one of these collective interests. Within schools, communitarians advocate that children should be encouraged to participate together in some shared processes by which they can experience creating the 'common good' for themselves. An education to understand the common good needs to encourage practices of cooperation, friendship, openness and participation. Other communitarians would argue that there can be no virtues worth teaching until citizens within a democracy have some recognition of a 'common good'. Nevertheless, the idea of the common good in education has intractable difficulties that communitarians have not yet addressed. Liberals believe that what counts as the good life is for each one to decide for themselves. However, the common good requires that education promote a greater balance between individual rights and the wider good of society and that no one should be excluded from the benefit of social development.

8 Religious schools are able to operate a strong version of the communitarian perspective

Many religious schools of all faiths are communities of place and memory and exhibit many of the features of the communitarian perspective on education. Many religious leaders also appear to support communitarian efforts and adopt aspects of communitarian thinking in explaining their own practices in education. Religious schools are generally strong communities, with their own narratives and virtue-centred approaches to education. They emphasize a communal ethos and believe that individual identity is not always a personal choice, but is formed by community and that religious tradition is constitutive of this community. The values and traditions inherent within these communities are not and need not be shared with everyone in the larger society. However, some communitarian writers who adopt a 'thick' idea of citizenship would not accept all religious schools as being communitarian in their practices, particularly any teaching of moral absolutism. Religious schools generally accept a 'thin' idea of citizenship and believe that the State should not interfere with their religious practices. They make a claim for cultural and religious identity within traditional, and often non-liberal, communities. The majority of communitarians adopt a conception of religion which is limited to the ethical field.

9 Many existing community-based education practices reflect the features of the communitarian perspective

Some communitarians would argue that there is a need for a focus on what makes schools good communities and less on what makes them efficient organizations. The case studies in this text illustrate many points of contact between the communitarian perspective on education and community schooling without any of these community schools explicitly discussing 'communitarianism'. Indeed, most of the teachers in these schools were not aware of much communitarian writing in the field. Nevertheless, each one of them had particular practices that illustrated certain communitarian features in education. These included democratic practices through citizenship education, devolved decision-making, taking the reality of community seriously, and promoting responsibilities towards society and a concern with promoting the common good.

10 Schools should adopt a more democratic structure of operating

Communitarianism generally says little about changing the capitalist structure of society, but in education many communitarians believe that schools should be managed in such a way as to encourage civic participation and democratic principles among young people. The principle of subsidiarity is expected to be taught and lived. The authority structures in schools would be non-hierarchical; communitarians would strongly advocate school councils and team approaches to full participation in joint decision-making, which includes a greater role in school decision-making for teachers and pupils. Power would be shared and members of the community would not be manipulated or alienated. There is a great deal of the 'ideal community' type of thinking in these recommendations, but how are schools to encourage democratic practices if their community structure is authoritarian?

Many of these themes appear to be drawn from traditional approaches in education and are therefore not new to the education profession. The current practices within the case studies show that many of these themes have been around for some time in educational discourse and practice. Each of the themes are therefore in need of further development by communitarians so as to express the particular communitarian character within each. Communitarian writing around these themes generally calls for the restoration of community and moral standards and it places an emphasis on the role of education to bring about personal and social change. Some believe that it is therefore a deeply conservative movement in education while others think it no more than a good deal of old-fashioned common sense dressed up as a grand new philosophy. Certainly there are few ideas which are entirely new in communitarian thinking, but it is also the case that strong versions of communitarianism have little in common with the general practice of the majority of schools in England and Wales. These ten themes represent much of the communitarian perspective on education and together they form an agenda for discussion.

However, communitarianism, like liberalism, is an ambiguous term. It is used by radicals and conservatives and means different things to different people. Despite all this, since the 1970s communitarianism has increasingly emerged as a central factor in contemporary socio-political debate, to the point that it can realistically be said that the communitarianism/liberal argument is crucial to that debate. Some communitarians like Charles Taylor would affirm their commitment to liberalism (Honderich 1995:143). Others like Michael Sandel offer it as an alternative, while Alasdair McIntyre views versions of it as another disguised contest of self-interested groups. Its adepts are a heterogeneous group from different disciplines, and the search for a working definition is ongoing and tentative.

Essentially, there are a number of tensions and unresolved issues within communitarian perspectives on education. The first is that there is no comprehensive theory of education from a communitarian perspective. Communitarian thinking on education has not advanced far enough to provide either a coherent 'end' for education or concrete 'means' by which we can achieve this end. This is not surprising when there are at least two schools within communitarian thinking; one which believes that communitarianism simply offers liberalism assistance in reforming itself and the other which believes that communitarianism is a distinctive philosophy or approach in itself. However, even the latter position, while being fundamentally communitarian, includes some liberal elements at both the theoretical and practical levels. In addition, it uses the rhetoric of liberalism in order to more effectively communicate ideas to a modern, largely liberal audience. There are, consequently, progressive as well as regressive potentialities within contemporary communitarian thinking that can lead to both radical and conservative possibilities. Communitarians often view individual autonomy as a threat to the community solidarity and identity whereas liberals consider individual autonomy vital for children to make their own decisions about the good life (see Wringe 1995). The moderate communitarian often seeks a balance between the autonomy-based and community-based arguments of liberals and other types of communitarians, rather than submerge their own communitarian thinking completely into the prevailing liberalism. This is perhaps what Etzioni means when he talks about restoring the 'balance' to liberal values. Another serious difficulty with communitarianism is that it is a public philosophy largely without a public, even if it is an important contribution to a growing discussion, conducted at present largely among academics. In addition, the central flaw in much communitarian thinking is that the only reason for acting non-selfishly it offers is selfishness – in that it is in your long-term interest to be altruistic. This is the central paradox of any communitarian idea which avoids teleology. The message is certainly an ambitious one concerned with restoring family, community and national core values, but will the message evoke change or even reach a majority of British citizens? Finally, the question must be asked whether or not the message is workable in schooling?

The answers are relatively easy. The message has already begun to evoke change since New Labour, and other political parties, have adopted aspects of communitarian thinking, and this is particularly seen in their political rhetoric. Tony Blair (1998:1) increasingly uses communitarian language in his political statements even if he does not use the word 'communitarian' itself. As he says: 'The Third Way is not an attempt to split the difference between Right and Left. It is about traditional values in a changed world'. And

> My politics are rooted in a belief that we can only realise ourselves
> as individuals in a thriving civil society, comprising strong families

and civic institutions buttressed by intelligent government. For most individuals to succeed, society must be strong. When society is weak, power and rewards go to the few not the many.

(Blair 1998:3)

While there has not emerged any workable communitarian blueprint for schooling, communitarian ideas on education are receiving increasing attention by politicians and policy-makers which consequently means that we need to be clear about what these communitarian ideas are and assess their implications for education in schools. This book has been a modest attempt to describe and outline some of these implications.

Communitarianism, despite its many difficulties, provides us with a positive focus for the discussion of contemporary educational ideas. The issues which are raised in this discussion are both relevant and significant for the progress of education within our school system. Teachers and schools are already addressing questions of character development and citizenship education as well as promoting the personal and social education of their pupils. However, this important task requires a great deal more support from local communities and from local and national government. Moreover, the means that central government uses to promote its agenda in education needs to be sensitive to what teachers already achieve in educating future citizens. Nevertheless, the government is right to encourage voluntary organizations to play a greater role in the public education system and to encourage the development of schools as base communities. Consequently, New Labour no longer seeks exclusive State control of all the different forms of schooling sponsored by the State. It is also directly as a result of New Labour engaging with communitarianism that the government has been able to connect the family and school much more closely together, a positive development the importance and significance of which churches, mosques, synagogues, and temples have long well understood. While publicly accepted standards of virtue have all but disappeared, it is within our many and diverse social settings conversing with strangers that perhaps we still recognize, as Roger Scruton (1997:114–15) writes:

> The virtues that inspire our admiration are also the qualities which preserve society, whether from external threat or from internal decay: courage and resolution in the face of danger; loyalty and decency in private life; justice and charity in the public sphere. At

different periods and in different conditions the emphasis shifts – virtue is malleable, shaped by material, spiritual and religious circumstances. Nevertheless, the constancy of the objects of human admiration is more significant than the local variations. The antique virtues of courage, prudence, wisdom, and temperance and justice, amplified by Christian charity and pagan loyalty, still form the core ideas of human excellence. It is these qualities that we admire, that we wish for in those we love, and hope to be credited with ourselves.

This goes beyond equating the 'good' only with pleasure. In conclusion, many communitarians appear to be utopians, that is, sincere men and women from academic think tanks who believe in an ideal social order. Unfortunately, in their zeal for attaining an ideal order they invariably run the danger of attempting to impose their own self-generated image of what society and therefore reality 'ought' to look like. Therefore, the problem with the communitarian agenda for education is that it promises more than exclusive State institutional schooling can possibly deliver.

References

Anderson, D. M. (1998) 'Communitarian approaches to the economy', in H. Giersch (ed.) *Merits and Limits of Markets*. Berlin Heidelbrey: New York.

Aquinas, T. (1991) *Summa Theologiae: A Concise Translation* (trans. T. McDermott). Methuen: London.

Arthur, J. (1995) *The Ebbing Tide*. Gracewing: Leominster.

Arthur, J. (1998) 'Communitarianism: what are the implications for education?', *Educational Studies*, 24(3): 353–68.

Atkinson, R. (1994) *The Common Sense of Community*. Demos: London.

Avineri, S. and De-Shelit, A. (eds) (1992) *Communitarianism and Individualism*.

Oxford University Press: Oxford.

Barber, B. R. (1991) 'A mandate for liberty: requiring education based community service', *The Responsive Community*, 1(2): 46–55.

Baumrind, D. (1973) 'The development of instrumental competence through socialization', in A. D. Pick (ed.) *Minnesota Symposium on Child Psychology, Volume 7*. University of Minnesota Press: Minnesota.

Baumrind, D. (1989) 'Rearing competent children', in W. Damon (ed.) *Child Development Today and Tomorrow*. Jossey-Bass: San Fransisco.

Beck, J. (1998) *Morality and Citizenship in Education*. Cassell: London.

Bell, D. A. (1993) *Communitarianism and its Critics*. Clarendon Press: Oxford.

Bellah, R. N. (1970) *Beyond Belief: Essays on Religion in a Post-traditional World*. Harper and Row: New York.

Bellah, R. N., Madsen, R., Sullivan, W. M., Swidler, A. and Tipton, S. M. (1985) *Habits of the Heart: Individualism and Commitment in American Life*. University of California Press: Berkeley.

References

Bellah, R. N., Madsen, R., Sullivan, W. M., Swidler, A. and Tipton, S. M. (1991) *The Good Society*. Knopf: New York.

Bentley, T. (1996) 'Learning beyond the classroom', *Demos Quarterly*, 9: 44–5.

Bentley, T. (1998) *Learning Beyond the Classroom: Education for a Changing World*. Routledge/Demos: London.

Blair, T. (1996) *New Britain – My Vision of a Young Country*. Fourth Estate: London.

Blair, T. (1998) *The Third Way: New Politics for the New Century*. Fabian Pamphlet: London.

Blunkett, D. (1997) *Excellence in Schools*, Department for Education: London.

Blustein, J. (1982) *Parents and Children – The Ethos of the Family*. Oxford University Press: New York.

Boswell, J. (1994) *Community and the Economy: The Theory of Public Co-operation*. Routledge: London.

Bradley, Y. (1996) 'Old wine, new wine-skins: reflections on metaphors for Christian organisation', *Journal of Christian Education*, 39(2): 37–45.

Bridges, D. and McLaughlin, T. H. (eds) (1994) *Education and the Market Place*. Falmer Press: London.

Bright, J. (1997) *Turning the Tide – Crime, Community and Prevention*. Demos: London.

Brooks, B. D. and Goble, F. G. (1997) *The Case for Character Education – the Role of the School in Teaching Values and Virtue*. Studio 4: Northridge, CA.

Bryk, A. S., Lee, V. E. and Holland, P. B. (1993) *Catholic Schools and the Common Good*. Harvard University Press: Cambridge, MA.

Buchanan, A. (1989) 'Assessing the Communitarian critique of Liberalism', *Ethics*, 99(4): 852–82.

Budziszewski, J. (1995) 'The problem with Communitarianism', *First Things*, 51: 22–6.

Burtonwood, N. (1998) 'Liberalism and Communitarianism: a response to two recent attempts to reconcile individual autonomy with group identity', *Educational Studies*, 24(3): 295–304.

Butcher, J. A., Henderson, G. P. and Smith, J. (eds) (1993) *Community and Public Policy*. Pluto Press: London.

Cambridge County Council (1990) *Learning Now – The Cambridgeshire Experience of Community Education*. Cambridge County Council: Cambridge.

146

Campbell, B. (1995) 'Old fogeys and angry young men: a critique of Communitarianism', *Soundings*, 1: 47–64.

Carey, S. (1992) 'Liberalism and Communitarianism: a misconceived debate', *Political Studies*, XL(2): 273–89.

Clarke, D. (1996) *Schools as Learning Communities: Transforming Education*. Cassell: London.

Clarke, F. (ed.) (1938) *Church, Community and State in Relation to Education*. George Allen and Unwin: London.

Close, F. P. (1993) 'The case for moral education', *The Responsive Community*, 4(1): 23–9.

Cochran, C. E. (1989) 'The thin theory of community: the communitarians and their critics', *Political Studies*, 37: 422–35.

Coleman, J. A. and Hoffer, T. (1987) *Public and Private High Schools: The Impact of Communities*. Basic Books: New York.

Coles, R. (1997) *The Moral Intelligence of Children*. Random House: New York.

Craig, A. (1995) Communitarianism: new left or new right? *Concept*, 5(3): 14–19.

Crick, B. (1962) In Defence of Politics. Weidenfeld and Nicholson: London.

Crouch, C. and Marquand, D. (1995) *Reinventing Collective Action*. Basil Blackwell: Oxford.

Dahl, R. (1995) 'Participation and the problem of civic understanding', in A. Etzioni (ed.) *Rights and the Common Good: A Communitarian Perspective*. St. Martin's Press: New York.

Daleney, C. F. (1994) *The Liberalism–Communitarian Debate*. Rowman and Littlefield Publishers: Lanham, MD.

Daley, M. (ed.) (1994) *Communitarianism: A New Public Ethics*. Wadsworth Publishing Company: Belmont, CA.

Damon, W. (1977) *The Social World of the Child*. Jossey-Bass: San Fransisco.

Damon, W. (1983) *Social and Personality Development – Infancy Through Adolescence*. W. W. Norton: New York.

Damon, W. (1988) *The Moral Child – Nurturing Children's Natural Moral Growth*. Free Press: New York.

Damon, W. (1995) *Greater Expectations – Overcoming the Culture of Indulgence in America's Homes and Schools*. Free Press: New York.

David, M. (1998) 'Editor's introduction', in M. David (ed.) *The Fragmented Family: Does It Matter?* Institute of Economic Affairs: London.

References

Davies, J. (1993) 'From household to family to individualism', in J. Davies (ed.) *The Family: Is It Just Another Lifestyle Choice?* Institute of Economic Affairs: London.

Demain, J. and Entwistle, H. (eds) (1998) *Beyond Communitarianism: Citizenship, Politics and Education*. Macmillan: London.

Dennis, N. and Erdos, G. (1993), *Families Without Fatherhood* (second edition, Foreword by A. H. Halsey). London: Institute of Economic Affairs.

Driver, S. and Martell, L. (1997) 'New Labour's Communitarianisms', *Critical Social Policy*, 17(3): 27–46.

Dworkin, R. (1978a) *Taking Rights Seriously*. Harvard University Press: Cambridge, MA.

Dworkin, R. (1978b) 'Philosophy and politics', in B. Magee (ed.) *Men of Ideas*. BBC: London.

Epstein, R. A. (1998) *Principles for a Free Society: Reconciling Individual Liberty With the Common Good*. Perseus Books: Reading, MA.

Etzioni, A. (1993) *The Parenting Deficit*. Demos: London.

Etzioni, A. (1995a) *The Spirit of Community: The Reinvention of American Society*. Touchstone: New York.

Etzioni, A. (1995b) *The Spirit of Community: Rights, Responsibilities and the Communitarian Agenda*. Harper Collins: London.

Etzioni, A. (ed.) (1995c) *Rights and the Common Good: A Communitarian Perspective*. St. Martin's Press: New York.

Etzioni, A. (ed.) (1995d) *New Communitarian Thinking: Persons, Virtues, Institutions and Community*. University of Virginia Press: Virginia.

Etzioni, A. (1997) *The New Golden Rule: Community and Morality in a Democratic Society*. Basic Books: New York.

Etzioni, A. (ed.) (1998) *The Essential Communitarian Reader*. Rowman and Littlefield Publishers: Lanham, MD.

Feinberg, W. (1995) 'The Communitarian challenges to Liberal social and educational theory', *Peabody Journal of Education*, 70(4): 34–55.

Ferri, E. (1993) *Britain's 33 Year Olds: The Fifth Follow-up to the National Child Development Study*. National Children's Bureau/ Economic and Social Research Council: London.

Fogelman, K. (1998) *Citizenship in Schools*. David Fulton: London.

Fowler, R. B. (1991) *The Dance with Community: The Contemporary Debate in American Political Thought*. University Press of Kansas: Lawrence, KS.

Frankel, P. and Miller, F. D. (eds) (1996) *The Communitarian Challenge to Liberalism*. Cambridge University Press: New York.

Frazier, E. and Lacey N. (1993) *The Politics of Community: A Feminist Critique of the Liberal–Communitarian Debate*. University of Toronto Press: Toronto.

Fried, C. (1983) 'Liberalism, community and the objectivity of values', *Harvard Law Review*, 96: 960–8.

Frohnen, B. (1992) 'Robert Bellah and the politics of civil religion', *Political Science Reviewer*, 21(Fall 1992): 148–218.

Frohnen, B. (1996) *The New Communitarians and the Crisis of Modern Liberalism*. University Press of Kansas: Lawrence, KS.

Fullinwider, R. K. (1995) 'Citizenship, individualism, and Democratic politics', *Ethics*, 105(3).

Galston, W. A. (1990) 'A Liberal–Democratic case for the two-parent family', in A. Etzioni (ed.) *The Essential Communitarian Reader*. Rowman and Littlefield: Lanham, MD.

Galston, W. A. (1991) *Liberal Purposes: Goods, Virtues and Diversity in the Liberal State*. Cambridge University Press: Cambridge.

Gardner, H. (1993) *The Unschooled Mind – How Children Think and How Schools Should Teach*. Fontana: London.

Garfinkle, N. (1998) *Moral Character Formation in the First Three Years*. Institute for Communitarian Policy Studies, The George Washington University: Washington DC.

Gayling, W. and Jennings, B. (1996) *The Perversion of Autonomy*. Free Press: New York.

Giddens, A. (1978) *Durkheim*. Fontana Press: London.

Giddens, A. (1998) *The Third Way – The Renewal of Social Democracy*. Polity Press: Cambridge.

Glendon, M. A. (1991) *Rights Talk: The Impoverishment of Political Discourse*. Free Press: New York.

Golby, M. (1997) 'Communitarianism and education', *Curriculum Studies*, 5(2): 125–39

Graham, J. and Bowling, B. (1995) *Young People and Crime – Home Office Research Study 145*. HMSO: London.

Grasso, K. L., Bradley, G. V. and Hunt, R. P. (1996) *Catholics, Liberalism and Communitarianism*. Rowman and Littlefield: New York.

Gray, J. (1993) *Beyond the New Right – Markets, Government and the Common Environment*. Routledge: London.

Gray, J. (1994) 'After the New Liberalism', *Social Research*, 61(3): 719–35.

Gray, J. (1995a) *Enlightenment's Wake – Politics and Culture at the Close of the Modern Age*. Routledge: London.

Gray, J. (1995b) *Berlin*. Fontana Press: London.

References

Gray, J. (1996) *After Social Democracy – Politics, Capitalism and the Common Life*. Demos: London.

Green, D. (1996) *Community Without Politics – A Market Approach to Welfare Reform*. Institute of Economic Affairs: London.

Griffith, R. (1998) *Educational Citizenship and Independent Learning*. Jessica-Kingsley: London.

Groome, T. H. (1996) 'What makes a school Catholic?', in T. H. McLaughlin, J. O'Keefe and B. O'Keeffe (eds) *The Contemporary Catholic School: Context, Identity and Diversity*. Falmer Press: London.

Guttman, A. (1987) *Democratic Education*. Princeton University Press: Princeton, NJ.

Guttman, A. (1995) 'Civic education and social diversity', *Ethics*, 105(3): 557–79.

Haldane, J. (1995) 'Educating: conserving tradition', in B. Almond (ed.) *Introducing Applied Ethics*. Blackwells: Oxford.

Haldane, J. (1996) 'Catholic education and Catholic identity', in T. H. McLaughlin, J. O'Keefe and B. O'Keeffe (eds) *The Contemporary Catholic School: Context, Identity and Diversity*. Falmer Press: London.

Halsey, A. H. (1972) *Educational Priority: EPA Problems and Policies*. HMSO: London.

Halstead, J. M. (1995) 'Voluntary Apartheid? Problems of schooling for religious and other minorities in democratic societies', *Journal of Philosophy of Education*, 29: 257–72.

Handy, C. and Aitken, R. (1986) *Schools as Organisations*. Penguin: Harmondsworth.

Hargreaves, D. H. (1982) *The Challenge for the Comprehensive School: Culture, Curriculum and Community*. Routledge and Kegan Paul: London.

Hargreaves, D. H. (1994) *The Mosaic of Learning – Schools and Teachers for the Next Millennium*. Demos: London.

Hartley, D. (1995) 'Communitarian anarchism and human nature, *Anarchist Studies*, 3: 145–64.

Haskey, J. (1998) 'Families: their historical context, and recent trends in the factors influencing their formation and dissolution', in M. David (ed.) *The Fragmenting Family: Does It Matter?* Institute of Economic Affairs: London.

Haste, H. (1996) 'Communitarianism and the social construction of morality', *Journal of Moral Education*, 25(1): 47–55.

Hauerwas, S. (1981) *A Community of Character: Towards a Constructive Christian Social Ethic*. University of Notre Dame Press: Notre Dame, IN.

Heater, D. (1990) *Citizenship: The Civic Ideal in World History, Politics and Education*. Longman: London.

Hewitt, P. and Leach, P. (1993) *Social Justice, Children and Families*. Institute for Public Policy Research: London.

Hirschi, T. (1969) *Causes of Delinquency*. Harvard University Press: Cambridge, MA.

Hirst, P. H. (1972) 'Christian education – a contradiction in terms', *Learning for Living*, 11(4): 6–10.

Holt, J. (1975) *Escape from Childhood*. Penguin: Harmondsworth.

Home Office (1998) *Supporting Families*. The Stationery Office: London.

Honderich, T. (ed.) (1995) *The Oxford Companion to Philosophy*. Oxford University Press: Oxford.

Hunt, T. (1996) 'It takes more than a village', *Demos Quarterly*, 9: 8–10.

Ingram, D. (1995) *Reason, History and Politics: The Communication Grounds for Legitimisation in the Modern Age*. State University of New York: New York.

Johnson, M. N. (1995) 'Nineteenth century agrarian populism and twentieth century communitarianism: points of contact', *Peabody Journal of Education*, 70(4): 86–104.

Jordan, B. (1989) *The Common Good: Citizenship, Morality and Self-interest*. Basil Blackwell: Oxford.

Keeble, R. W. J. (1981) *Community and Education*, National Youth Bureau: Leicester.

Keys, M. (1996) 'Personal dignity and the common good: a twentieth-century Thomistic dialogue', in K. L. Grasso, G. V. Bradley and R. P. Hunt (eds) *Catholics, Liberalism and Communitarianism*. Rowman and Littlefield: New York.

Kiernan, K. (1998), 'Family change: issues and implications', in M. David (ed.) *The Fragmenting Family: Does It Matter?* Institute of Economics Affairs: London.

Killick, R. (1996), 'The family problem', in D. Hayes (ed.) *Debating Education: Issues for the New Millennium*. Canterbury Christ Church College: Canterbury, Kent.

Kymlicka, W. (1993) 'Community', in R. E. Goodin and P. Pettit (eds) *A Companion to Political Philosophy*. Blackwells: Oxford.

Leach, P. (1989) *Your Baby and Child from Birth to Age Five*. Knopf: New York.

Leadbeater, C. and Goss, S. (1998) *Civic Entrepreneurship*. Demos/Public Management Foundation: London.

References

Leming, J. S. (1994) 'Character education and the creation of community', *The Responsive Community*, 4(4): 49–57.

Likona, T. (1991) *Educating for Character – How Our Schools Can Teach Respect and Responsibility*. Bantam: New York.

Lynn, R. (1992) 'Self-control: the family as the source of "conscience"', in D. Anderson (ed.) *The Loss of Virtue: Moral Confusion and Social Disorder in Britain and America*. Social Affairs Unit: London.

McClelland, A. V. (1991) 'Education in modern Catholicism: Vatican II and after', in A. Hastings (ed.) *25 Years After Vatican II*. SPCK: London.

Macedo, S. (1995) 'Liberal civic education and religious fundamentalism', *Ethics*, 103(3): 468–96.

McIntyre, A. (1967) *A Short History of Ethics*. Routledge: London.

McIntyre, A. (1981) *After Virtue: A Study in Moral Theory*. Duckworth: London.

McIntyre, A. (1987) 'The idea of an educated public', *Education and Values: The Richard Peters Lectures*. Institute of Education: London.

MacIntyre, A. (1988) *Whose Justice? Which Rationality?* Duckworth: London.

MacIntyre, A. (1990) *First Principles, Final Ends and Contemporary Philosophical Issues*. Marquette University Press: Milwaukee, WI.

McKinstry, L. (1997) *Turning the Tide: A Personal Manifesto for Modern Britain*. Michael Joseph: London.

McLaughlin, T. H. (1992) 'Citizenship, diversity and education: a philosophical perspective', *Journal of Moral Education*, 21(3): 235–50.

MacMurray, J. (1992) *The Conditions of Freedom*. Humanities: New York.

Manzoor-ul-Hague (1993) 'The Qur'anic model of education', *Muslim Education Quarterly*, 10(2): 35–43.

Marenbon, J. (1997) *Answering the Communitarian Challenge*. Politeia: London.

Miles, R. (1994) *The Children We Deserve – Love and Hate in the Making of the Family*. Harper Collins: London.

Miller, D. (1990) 'The resurgence of political theory', *Political Studies*, 38: 421–37.

Mitchell, B. (1995) 'The distinction of powers: how Church and State divide us', *Theologies and Moral Concern, Religion in Public Life*, 29: 1–20.

Morgan, P. (1995) *Farewell to the Family: Public Policy and Family Breakdown in Britain and the USA*. Institute of Economic Affairs: London.

Morgan, P. (1996) *Who Needs Parents: The Effects of Childcare and Early Education on Children in Britain and the USA*. Institute of Economic Affairs: London.

Morgan, P. (1998) 'An endangered species?', in M. David (ed.) *The Fragmenting Family: Does It Matter?* Institute of Economic Affairs: London.

Mulhall, S. and Swift, A. (1996) *Liberals and Communitarians*. Blackwells: Oxford.

Mussen, P. and Eisenberg-Berg, N. (1977) *Roots of Sharing, Sharing and Helping: The Development of Pro-social Behavior in Children*. W. H. Freeman: San Francisco.

Nash, R. J. (1997) *Answering the 'Virtuecrats': A Moral Conversation on Character Education*. Teachers College Press: Columbia University.

National Curriculum Council (1990) *Curriculum Guidance 8: Education for Citizenship*. National Curriculum Council: York.

Neal, P. and Paris, D. (1990) 'Liberalism and the Communitarian critique: a guide for the perplexed', *The Canadian Journal of Political Science*, 23(3): 419–39.

Nisbet, R. (1953) *The Quest for Community*. Lanham: San Francisco, CA.

Novak, M. (1989) *Free Persons and the Common Good*. Madison Books: New York.

Nozick, R. (1977) *Anarchy, State and Utopia*. Basic Books: New York.

O'Hear, A. (1992) 'Respect and the dangers of an unfettered "critical spirit" in education', in D. Anderson (ed.) *The Loss of Virtue: Moral Confusion and Social Disorder in Britain and America*. Social Affairs Unit: London.

Oldfield, A. (1990) *Citizenship and Community: Civic Republicanism and the Modern State*. Routledge: London.

O'Neill, J. (1994) *The Missing Child in Liberal Theory – Towards a Covenant Theory of Family, Welfare, and the Civic State*. University of Toronto Press: Toronto.

Osler, A. and Starkey, H. (1996) *Teaching for Citizenship in the New Europe*. Trentham Books: Stoke on Trent.

Peters, M. and Marshall, J. (eds) (1989) *Individualism and Community – Education and Social Policy in the Postmodern Condition*. Falmer Press: London.

Phillips, D. L. (1993) *Looking Backward: – A Critical Appraisal of Communitarian Thought*. Princeton University Press: Princeton, NJ.

Phillips, M. (1994) 'The father of Tony Blair's big idea', *Observer*, 24 July 1994: 27.

References

Phillips, M. (1996) *All Must Have Prizes*. Little, Brown and Company: London.

Popenoe, D. (1994) 'The roots of declining social virtues: family, community and the need for a "Natural Communities Policy"', in D. Popenoe, A. Norton and B. Maley (eds) *Shaping Social Virtues*. Centre for Independent Studies: St. Leonards, NSW, Australia.

Prior, D., Stewart, J. and Walsh, K. (1995) *Citizenship: Rights, Community, and Participation*. Pitman: London.

Pugh, G., De'Ath, E. and Smith, C. (1994) *Confident Parents, Confident Children*. National Children's Bureau: London.

Raeder, L. C. (1989) 'Liberalism and the common good: a Heyekian perspective on Communitarianism', *The Independent Review: The Journal of Political Economy*, Spring, 2(4): 519–36.

Rasmussen, D. B. (1990) *Universalism v Communitarianism: Contemporary Debates in Ethics*. MIT Press: Boston, MA.

Raths, L., Harmin, M. and Simon, S. (1966) *Values and Teaching – Working with Children in the Classroom*. Merrill: Columbus, OH.

Rauner, M. (1997) 'Citizenship in the curriculum: the globalisation of civics education in anglophone Africa 1955–1995', in C. McNeeley (ed.) *Public Rights, Public Rules: Constituting Citizens in the World Polity and National Policy*. New York: Garland Publishing.

Ravitch, D. (1991) 'Pluralism v particularism in American education', *The Responsive Community*, 1(2): 32–45.

Rawls, J. (1972) *A Theory of Justice*. Harvard University Press: Harvard, MA.

Ree, H. (1985) *Educator Extraordinary*. London: Peter Owen.

Rentoul, J. (1995) *Tony Blair*. Little, Brown and Company: London.

Ringen, S. (1998) *The Family in Question*. Demos: London.

Rogoff, B. (1990) *Apprenticeship in Thinking – Cognitive Development in Social Context*. Oxford University Press: New York.

Rosario, J. R. and Franklin, B. M. (1994) 'National service and the ideal of community: a commentary on what you can do for your country', *Journal of Education Policy*, 9(3): 267–75.

Rosenblith, J. and Sims-Knight, J. (1989) *In the Beginning: Development in the First Two Years*. Sage: Newbury Park, CA.

Rousseau, J. J. (1974) *Emile* (trans. B. Foxley). Dent: London.

Rutter, M., Mortimer, P. and Maugham, B. (1979) *Fifteen Thousand Hours: Secondary Schools and their Effects on Children*. Open Books: London.

Ryan, K. and McLean, G. F. (1987), *Character Development in School and Beyond*. Praeger: New York.

Sacks, J. (1997) *The Politics of Hope*. Jonathan Cape: London.

Sandel, M. J. (1984) *Liberalism and its Critics*. Basil Blackwell: Oxford.

SCAA (1996–1997) *National Forum for Values in Education and the Community*, unpublished draft. Schools Curriculum and Assessment Authority: London.

Scruton, R. (1997) *An Intelligent Person's Guide to Philosophy*. Duckworth: London.

Sears, A. (1996) 'Something different to everyone: conceptions of citizenship and citizenship education', *Canadian and International Education*, 25(2): 1–16.

Selbourne, D. (1997) *The Principle of Duty – An Essay on the Foundations of Civic Society*. London: Abacus.

Selzinck, P. (1987) 'The idea of a Communitarian morality', *The California Law Review*, 75: 445–63.

Snauwaert, D. T. (1995) 'International ethics, community, and civic education', *Peabody Journal of Education*, 70(4): 119–38.

Stradling, R. (1987) 'Political Education and Politicization in Britain: A Ten Year Perspective'. Paper presented at the International Round Table Conference of the research Committee on Political Education of the International Political Science Association, Ostkolleg der Bundeszentrale fur Politische Bilding, Koln, 9–13 March 1987.

Tam, H. (1996) 'Education and the Communitarian movement', *Pastoral Care in Education*, 14(3): 28–31.

Tam, H. (ed.) (1996) *Punishment, Excuses and Moral Development*. Avebury: Aldershot.

Tam, H. (1998) *Communitarianism: A New Agenda for Politics and Citizenship*. Macmillan Press: London.

Tate, N. (1998) *'What is Education For?'* King's College, London, Fifth Annual Education Lecture, London, 30 November 1998.

Taylor, C. (1989) *Sources of Self: The Making of the Modern Identity*. Harvard University Press: Cambridge, MA.

Thayer-Bacon, B. J. (1998) *Philosophy Applied to Education: Nurturing Democratic Community in the Classroom*. Merrill: New Jersey.

Theobald, P. (1998) *A Place for Rural Schools: A Communitarian Perspective*. Westview: Boulder, CO.

Theobald, P. and Snauwaert, D. T. (eds) (1995) 'Education and the Liberal Communitarian debate', *Peabody Journal of Education*, 70(4).

Tooley, J. (1995) *Disestablishing the School – Debunking Justifications for State Intervention in Education*. Avebury: Aldershot.

Tooley, J. (1996) *Education Without the State*. Institute of Economic Affairs: London.

References

Vallely, P. (1998) *The New Politics*. SCM: London.

Waite, L. J. (1996) 'Social science finds: "marriage matters"', *The Responsive Community*, 6(3): 26–35.

Wallach, J. R. (1987) 'Liberals, Communitarians and the tasks of political theory', *Political Theory*, 15(4): 581–611.

Walzer, M. (1990) 'The Communitarian critique of Liberalism', *Political Theory*, 18(1): 6–23.

West, E. G. (1994) *Education and the State – A Study in Political Economy*. Liberty Press: Indianapolis, IN.

Wilcox, B. (1997) 'Schooling, school improvement and the relevance of Alasdair McIntyre', *Cambridge Journal of Education*, 27(2): 249–60.

Wildasky, B. (1991) 'Can you teach morality in public schools?', *The Responsive Community*, 2(1): 46–54.

Willetts, D. (1991) *Happy Families – Four Points to a Conservative Family Policy*. Centre for Policy Studies: London.

Willets, D. (1994) 'Civic conservatism', in J. Gray and D. Willets (eds) *Is Conservatism Dead?* Profile: London.

Willetts, D. (1996) *Blair's Guru – An Examination of Labour Rhetoric*. Centre of Policy Studies: London.

Wills, G. (1990) *Under God: Religion and American Politics*. Simon and Schuster: New York.

Wilson, J. Q. (1993) *The Moral Sense*. Free Press: New York.

Wilson, J. Q. (1997) *On Character*. Free Press: New York.

Wringe, C. (1995) 'Two challenges to the notion of rational autonomy and their educational implications', *Educational Philosophy and Theory*, 27(2): 49–63.

Young, I. M. (1994) *Intersecting Voices: Dilemmas of Gender, Political Philosophy, and Policy*. Princeton University Press: Princeton, NJ.

Young, M. and Halsey, A. H. (1995) *Family and Community Socialism*. Institute for Public Policy Research: London.

Index

157